Medicine
for the
Backcountry

2nd Edition

by Buck Tilton, M.S, and
Frank Hubbell, D. O.

Illustrations by
Marc Bohne

D0201376

ICS BOOKS, INC.
Merrillville, Indiana

Medicine for the Backcountry 2nd Edition

Copyright © 1994 by Buck Tilton, M.S. & Frank Hubbell, D.O.

10 9 8 7 6 5 4 3 2 1

Printed in the U.S.A.

All ICS titles are printed on 50% recycled paper from pre-consumer waste. All sheets are processed without using acid.

Published by:

ICS Books, Inc.

1370 E. 86th Place

Merrillville, IN 46410

800-541-7323

Co- Published in Canada by:

VANWELL PUBLISHING LTD.

1 Northrup Crescent

P.O. Box 2131,

St. Catharines, Ontario L2M 6P5.

800-661-6136

Library of Congress Cataloging-in-Publication Data

Tilton, Buck.
    Medicine for the backcountry / Buck Tilton, M.S. and Frank Hubbell, D.O. --
2nd edition
    p. cm.
    Includes index.
    ISBN 1-57034-002-1 :
    1. Mountaineering injuries. 2. First aid in illness & injury.
I. Hubbell, Frank. II. Title.
RC1220.M6T55 1994   94-11619
616.02'52--dc20   CIP

Contents

To MELISSA GRAY with great love,
For her unshakable friendship and
Matchless companionship,
For her wilderness wisdom,
For her wondrous care
That exemplifies "good medicine."

Preface to the Second Edition

Five years have passed since the winter this book was first written. A new log cabin holds back sub-zero temperatures, and these words glow on a new computer screen. Yesterday's stillness has been altered by wind rustling icily through the spruce, and dawn turns the morning sky from gray to faded rose. Ever changing, life is dynamic . . . and, ever changing, medicine is dynamic. If you have already read the first edition, you'll find many differences and many additions in the book you hold. If you're reading for the first time, you have a book as up-to-date as possible.

Five years, and we've learned much, and we've enjoyed even more. Reviewers have been kind and readers have lavished praise. But the great reward has been the response of literally thousands of our full-of-wonder students who have turned words into care for patients. "All interest in disease and death," wrote Thomas Mann, "is only another expression of interest in life."

Preface

Rugged miles and tired muscles, the cutting edge of an icy wind, loose footing through a black night: all are part of providing backcountry emergency care. Staying warm is a matter of the clothes you wear, the food you eat, the water you carry on your back. There are never too many to bear the litter, but always more than enough opinions about the best way to go. Your creativity and determination are directly proportional to your success. When the vitals are stable, the splints secure, your adrenaline rush ebbs, but the work has just begun.

We want to do it because we love the wild places, and we feel compassion for the wonderful and crazy people who go there. We want to preserve the lives of both. The way of the unrestrained river becomes our way, the endless movement, the steady flow, the path of least resistance.

From this book you may acquire knowledge that will help you ease pain and save lives, but it is merely information. Everything presented here should be tempered with the wisdom that comes from experience. Your greatest skill is your ability to reason and judge, your best piece of equipment is your brain. To come from your training with a pocketful of pat answers is to miss the point. No two backcountry situations are ever the same. Here is a written foundation to build on. Finding the best way to do something is not as important as finding a method that works.

More important than your selection of a text is your choice of instructors. A team rarely exceeds the strength of its leader, or a course the ability of its teacher. Look for someone who can translate windsong and the moan of an aching back into understandable words and experiences.

Study first to know yourself, second to accept yourself, and third to discipline yourself toward a higher level of performance. Be silent and listen. Grow aware. When you have learned to change what you know into perfect patient care in the wilderness, your journey has begun.

Chapter 1
Primary Assessment

Dancing across the high mountain meadow in a glistening swirl of clarity, the South Fork of the Little Wind River blocked the hikers from their chosen campsite. They could see it lying in the shade of tall pines, a flat spot begging for a couple of tents. Dropping their backpacks, four of them began to patiently remove their socks and replace their boots, preparing to wade. The fifth sized up the spacing of rocks, judging the feasibility of a hopping dash to the other side.

Making his decision, the impatient dasher tightened his hipbelt and started across. The last rock before dry land was wet from periodic surges of the river. When the backpacker's foot fell there, it found no purchase. Up went his feet and down went his lower back, thumping heavily against the rock, the pack absorbing some of the blow. He crawled the remaining few feet to shore, and collapsed on his side. When his friends waded hurriedly to his assistance, the damaged hiker was unable to rise, complaining of severe lower back pain.

It was 14 miles to the nearest road, which was dirt and seldom used. It was late September, the water was very cold and the ground wasn't much better. Darkness was on the verge of settling down. It was time for an application of *backcountry medicine*.

This situation calls for much more than *first aid*. First aid is a part of it, but its intention is, and always has been, stabilization of the injured person until he can be transferred to a medical facility for definitive care. Even highly-skilled pre-hospital personnel are trained to respond in the context of short-term care of the injured and sick.

The wilderness requires long-term care in medicine, just as it insists on a higher level of self-sufficiency in all areas of living beyond the amenities of civilization. In a remote geographical environment, the time/distance relationship of the incident and a medical center is one of three ingredients that add to first aid. The second is the severity of the environment: cold, wet, wind, heat, darkness, rough terrain, shortages of potable water and more. And finally, the lack of specialized equipment often demands creative improvisation on the part of the rescuer.

Survey the Scene

Doubled up in pain, unable to move, the hasty backpacker lay deep in the Wind River Mountains, obviously hurt. But there was no immediate danger... or was there? What should you be thinking about as you approach this person? What is your first concern for your injured friend?

If your answer was Airway, Breathing, and Circulation (the ABC's), you have made a mistake, perhaps a serious one! Your first thoughts at any rescue scene should be toward your own safety, and the safety of others with you.

MAXIM:

NEVER CREATE A SECOND VICTIM

The worst thing you can do at any scene is create a second victim. A quick check for immediate hazards needs to be made. When an accident occurs, whether someone is injured or not, the result is invariably a degree of confusion. Disorganization promotes the chance of further injury and delays the start of adequate patient care.

In the Winds, those who hurried to the rescue wore heavy packs and walked on slippery rocks. September darkness brought a plunge in temperature. Everyone was damp from a sweaty hike. The victim was drenched in icy water, and had already begun to tremble.

It is difficult to find a well-managed scene without a manager. Someone needs to take charge! If a leader has not been pre-arranged, the time it requires to choose one may be the most valuable moments in the rescue. The leader needs to maintain a high level of objectivity. Staying objective will allow the leader to check the accident area for acute or subtle dangers, which includes checking the approach to the victim for safety. Leadership involves assigning appropriate tasks to everyone, gathering information to make a plan of action, and observing to insure nothing is left undone.

Take a deep, calming breath. Take charge of yourself first. If you are alone, order the tasks that must be done, and get to work. Don't just stand there.

We are accustomed to thinking of getting the maximum good out of a minimum of equipment. We learn to look at everything as a potential asset: pack frames, sleeping pads, bandanas, tent poles. All of these items share the characteristic of being inanimate. It takes a person to make them perform a needed function. People are the most valuable resource. They can think, plan, put up a tent, make hot tea, build a splint, carry a litter. When a second victim is created, the party not only has twice as many problems to deal with, but also one less of its most valuable resource. The situation is more than twice as difficult!

Train yourself to check first for a safe scene. Pause as you approach the victim, look to the leader for organization, ask: "Is this safe?" It usually is, but the one time it isn't, all the difference in success or failure can be made if you notice the danger.

Primary Survey (ABCDE)
Airway & Breathing

Breathing is a fantastic process. Contraction of the diaphragm and intercostal muscles causes the size of the space inside the chest to increase. To fill the space, air rushes in through the nose or mouth, past the throat, down the trachea (windpipe) to the bronchi, where it goes either right or left, through bronchioles of ever-diminishing size to the alveoli. In the alveoli, oxygen passes easily through a semi-permeable membrane and into the blood. Carbon dioxide leaves the blood, collecting in the alveoli. When the muscles relax, the chest cavity decreases in size and the air is pushed out, expelling the carbon dioxide.

Everything works fine as long as the pathway of the air is not obstructed. If the scene is safe, your next concern is your patient's airway.

A simple question, "Are you okay?" often elicits a response such as, "No, you idiot, didn't you see me fall?" This may or may not be an appropriate answer, but at least your patient can breathe. If they do not respond, you must get your ear down near the opening of the airway, and LOOK, LISTEN and FEEL for air exchange.

The most common obstruction of the airway in an unconscious victim is the tongue. Deep unconsciousness can cause it and the epiglottis to fall back across the throat. An easy method for opening the airway is pushing down on the forehead while lifting the chin—the head-tilt chin-lift method. Open the mouth of your patient, listen again for air movement and wet breathing sounds, and look for blood, vomit, or other obstructions to breathing that might fill the mouth. If there is a suspicion of neck injury, the airway can be opened with a lift of the jaw without movement of the neck—the jaw-thrust method.

Figure 1-1
Opening an airway with
head-tilt chin-lift method.

HEAD TILT CHIN LIFT

On a good day, patients will start to breathe when you open the airway. If they don't, it means either the airway is obstructed by an object other than their tongue, or they are in respiratory arrest. Pinching their nose closed and sealing your mouth over theirs (use of a rescue mask would be even better) allows you to breathe air into their lungs. If it won't go in, try repositioning the head, and attempt a second breath. No go? A foreign body airway obstruction can often be cleared out by straddling the patients' thighs and manually and forcefully thrusting their abdomen up toward their chest. Keep your hands low, away from the lower end of their sternum where the xiphoid process waits to be broken off. Thrust up to five times, and check their mouth with a finger sweep to see if you have dislodged the object. Try another breath. If the breath won't go in, try up to five more thrusts. Continue until it works.

Figure 1-2
Opening an airway with the jaw-thrust method.

If at any time the patient starts to vomit, roll him or her quickly onto their side to allow gravity to do the job of draining the airway clear. Use a finger sweep to help clear the airway, if necessary.

Victims of respiratory arrest need to have someone breathe for them, at least once every five seconds, until they start to breathe on their own. Mouth-to-mouth or mouth-to-nose breathing will work better if you have taken the time to practice in anticipation of an emergency.

NOTE: Rescue breathing is a safer bet in terms of your own personal health if you use a pocket rescue mask.

Circulation

The heart beats. The blood goes round and round, leaving the heart through arteries, passing through capillaries, and returning through veins. Arteries carry de-oxygenated blood to the lungs, where it washes over the alveoli, discarding CO_2 and picking up fresh O_2. Arteries carry oxygenated blood to all of the body's seventy-five trillion or so cells. Every cell needs the oxygen to survive.

When your heart stops beating, you are clinically dead. In approximately four to six minutes, without oxygen, brain cells, the ones most easily affected by an O_2 shortage, begin to die. It doesn't take long for a significant number of brain cells to die, leaving you biologically dead.

During the few minutes between clinical and biological death, it is sometimes possible to interrupt the dying process and resuscitate the victim. It is, therefore, very important to assess the circulation of your patient as soon as possible. You can do that quickly by pressing several of your fingers lightly into the hollow below the angle of your patient's jaw. There you should feel the carotid pulse.

Figure 1-3
Checking the pulse at the carotid artery.

If you cannot find the pulse, it is time to begin the process of chest compression and mouth-to-mouth ventilation known as cardiopulmonary resuscitation (CPR). If you do not know how to perform CPR, you will very likely be wishing you had taken the time to learn.

ONE-RESCUER ADULT CPR
1. Assess responsiveness with a gentle shake and a shout.
2. No response? (Near a phone—call 911.) Turn patient onto back, if necessary, while supporting the head and neck.
3. Open the airway and assess breathing.
4. No breathing? Give two slow full ventilations, watching for the chest to rise and allowing it to passively relax between breaths.
5. Feel for a carotid pulse.

6. No pulse? Begin chest compressions by placing one hand on the lower third of the sternum, placing your other hand over the first, keeping your arms straight, and pressing down 1-1/2 to 2 inches. Depress the sternum 15 times at a rate of 80-100 compressions per minute (a little more than once a second).
7. After every 15 compressions, give 2 slow full ventilations.
8. After four cycles of 15:2 (approximately one minute), recheck for a pulse. If no pulse, continue with 15:2.

Severe Bleeding

Once you reach your adult size, you probably have 5-6 liters of blood circulating in your body. Losing about 10% of it will cause you to feel weak and lightheaded. Loss of another 10% to 15% will result in inadequate perfusion of your tissues (see *Shock*) leaving you incapacitated until you can manufacture more blood. As blood loss approaches the 50% mark, the likelihood of death grows greater and greater.

It is important to check patients quickly for severe loss of blood. A visual scan is often enough. But sometimes blood loss can be hidden in bulky clothing and water-resistant shells. Check inside clothing if there is any possibility of severe bleeding. Heavy blood loss can also disappear into the environment upon which your patient is lying. Look underneath them in snow, sand, rocks, and any ground cover that may be hiding large amounts of blood.

Severe blood loss should be stopped immediately with pressure from your hand directly on the wound. It's better to place something sterile on the wound first, but in an emergency grab a shirt, a bandana, or anything available. Direct pressure can be augmented by elevating the wound above the patient's heart.

NOTE: Your personal health has a better chance of staying good if you put on protective gloves before contacting blood, or any other body fluid, and if you wash your hands thoroughly afterwards.

Once pressure has been applied, it should be maintained until clotting is well established. If someone can get a bulky sterile dressing it can be tied firmly in place to maintain pressure. This pressure dressing should be monitored to make sure adequate circulation is getting past the pressure. You don't want it to become a tourniquet.

In some cases it isn't feasible to apply direct pressure. Perhaps the area is too large to compress, or the pressure causes your patient too much pain. Bleeding can be discouraged by putting pressure on pressure points. These are places where arteries are close enough to the surface to squash them against bone and reduce the flow of blood. The handiest two are

1) the brachial pressure point, anywhere inside the upper arm, and 2) the femoral, which lies along an imaginary line between the iliac crest (the high point of the pelvis) and the center of the groin. Pressure points can also be used as an adjunct to direct pressure.

Avoid direct pressure on open head wounds because unstable bones might be pressed into the brain. Use a bulky absorbent pad and press lightly on the wound. Avoid direct pressure on open neck wounds near the patient's airway, which might be pressed shut. Pinch the wound closed with your fingers.

Tourniquets cut off all blood flow and are used as last resorts. Flat material, about four inches wide, works best. It should be placed close to the wound, but above the elbow or knee. Any stick can be used to snug the material down until blood flow stops. Loosen the tourniquet slowly after approximately 10 minutes to see if bleeding has stopped. Retighten if necessary, but leave the tourniquet in place no longer than is required.

Disability: The Cervical Spine

Fractures and dislocations of the seven bones that make up the neck, the cervical spine, can be repaired. Damage to the spinal cord running through them can not. The result of spinal cord damage in the cervical region is usually quadriplegia or death. For that reason we take the primary precaution of keeping the head and neck as still as possible if there is any suspicion of cervical spine injury.

Our level of suspicion should be very high if the patient is unconscious or injured as a result of an accident which throws the neck forcefully out of alignment (falls from a height, sudden high-speed stops, blows to the head). The patient may or may not complain of neck pain. Sometimes spinal injuries ruin the life of a victim hours after the accident through subsequent swelling and movement.

Do not let fear of spinal injury blind you to more immediate threats to life. If the scene is not safe, the patient may need to be carefully moved (see *Spinal Cord Injury Management*). If the airway is not open, grasp the sides of your patient's head firmly, and with steady, gentle motion, attempt to align the head and neck with the rest of the body. Manual stability should be maintained until mechanical stabilization can be improvised (see *Spinal Cord Injury Management*).

MAXIM:

WHEN IN DOUBT, TREAT THE WORST POSSIBLE INJURY

Exposure/Environment

Injuries are often buried in clothing and can't be treated properly, or even successfully sometimes, unless they are exposed. This may require cutting away or taking off clothing. But keep in mind, in the backcountry, that removal of clothing will further expose the patient to the environment: cold, wet, wind, etc. Expose the patient with care and discrimination, if at all possible.

The goal of the primary assessment is a patient who is initially safe from immediate threats to life. After being stabilized and moved to the warm security of a tent and sleeping bag, our Wind River victim lay for four uncomfortable days until a helicopter evacuation was accomplished. His recovery was eventually complete.

The Barehanded Principles:

PRIMARY ASSESSMENT

1. Check the scene for safety.

2. Use protective gloves and a pocket rescue mask.

3. Manually stabilize the cervical spine.

4. Ensure an airway and breathing.

5. Ensure the heart is circulating blood.

6. Stop any severe bleeding.

7. Expose injuries as needed, but beware overexposure to the environment.

Chapter 2
Secondary Assessment

It was late afternoon, and northern New Hampshire grew chilly. With numbing hands, the climber on Cannon Mountain lost control and took a leader fall of approximately sixty feet. Swinging like a pendulum he crashed back-first into the granite wall. Conscious, but unable to continue up or down, he was skillfully lowered to the ground by his partner, who ran for help.

When we arrived with a carrying team, he complained of head and chest pain, and had forgotten the specifics of what happened. Once he was stabilized in the litter, we started out slowly, picking our way over the darkening pile of rubble at the foot of the route.

"How's the ride?" Frank asked our patient for the tenth time. But now he failed to get the irritated answer he expected. We stopped for a quick reassessment. The injured climber responded sluggishly to a painful stimulus. His respirations were deeper than the last check, and more labored. There was a significant increase in blood pressure. Frank voiced all our concerns: "We're losing him."

Picking up the pace, stumbling in the bobbing light of head lamps, we hurried as best we could, reaching the trail head in less time than we imagined possible. An exhausted team watched the ambulance pull briskly away.

The hospital at Littleton found nine ribs fractured near the spine and, more importantly, a swollen brain. Our notice of his deteriorating condition and the following rush to the road probably, said the attending physician, made the difference between death and the climber's fortunate recovery.

The Physical Exam

When the immediate threats to life have been controlled, our assessment needs to extend systematically over the entire patient, evaluating the extent of the known injuries, and looking for unsuspected damage hidden by the pain and the obvious. The situation will determine the sequence and thoroughness of this examination. But all patients deserve a complete, hands-on, head-to-toe check. (In small children, you may wish to go toe-to-head, gaining their confidence before attacking their vulnerable head and chest.)

General guidelines for the patient exam include:

1) Gentle but firm palpation (feeling) of all relevant body parts, looking for obvious damage, pain responses, swelling, deformities and abnormalities.

2) Moving the patient as little as possible, and not aggravating known injuries.

3) When necessary, cutting away clothing to make suspected injuries visible.

4) Communicating with patients through the entire process, even if they appear unconscious. They are the questions, and they are the answers!

Specifically move from head to toe, *Looking, Asking* and *Feeling* (LAF) for the signs and symptoms of problems. It is a kind way to LAF at them.

HEAD: Looking for damage, discoloration, and blood or fluid draining from ears, nose and mouth. Asking about loss of consciousness, pain or any abnormal sensations. Feeling for lumps or other deformities.

NECK: Looking for obvious damage or deviance in the trachea. Asking about pain and discomfort. Feeling along the cervical spine for a pain response.

CHEST: Compress the ribs from both sides, as if squeezing a bird cage, keeping your hands wide to prevent the possibility of too much direct pressure on fractures. Look for damage or deformities. Ask about pain. Feel for instability.

ABDOMEN: With hands spread wide, press gently on the abdomen. Look for damage. Ask about pain and discomfort. Feel for rigidity, distention or muscle spasms.

BACK: Slide your hands under the patient, palpating as much of the spine as possible.

PELVIS: Cup the iliac crests with your hands, pressing gently down and pulling toward the mid-line of the body. Ask about pain. Feel for instability.

LEGS: With your hands surrounding each leg one at a time, run from the groin down to the toes, squeezing as you go. Note especially if there is a lack of circulation, sensation or motion in the toes.

SHOULDERS and ARMS: One at a time, with hands wide, squeeze each shoulder and run down the arms to the fingers. Check for circulation, sensation and motion in the fingers.

At some point, a written note of all possible injuries should be kept. Don't let known injuries keep you from a thorough examination. Soon you will be treating all suspected damage.

The Vital Signs

An accurate measurement of a body's vital functions do not tell you what is wrong with your patient. But they do relate how well your patient is doing. The second set of vital signs is more important than the first set. And the third more important than the second. Circumstances will dictate how often the signs are taken, but the change over time is the key to using vital signs in long-term patient care. A constant monitoring of your patients should be maintained until they are "out of the woods." And remember: Do not isolate on one vital sign, but take them as a whole picture.

Level of Consciousness

A normal level of consciousness allows your patient to answer intelligently in a way that tells you if he or she is oriented in person, place, time and event. They should know who they are, where they are, generally what time it is, and what happened. The LOC is the easiest sign to assess, and the first to change. It can be recorded easily using the AVPU scale, which assigns the patient a letter grade from alert to unresponsive.

ALERT: Patients seem normal and answer intelligently questions about person, place, time and event. They know essentially what happened to them.

VERBAL: Patients are not alert, but they do respond in some way when spoken to.

PAIN: Patients do not react to verbal stimuli, but they do react to being pinched or rubbed in sensitive areas.

UNRESPONSIVE: Patients do not respond to stimuli.

Pulse

In the *primary assessment* you noticed a pulse at the carotid artery, assuring yourself your patient had blood being pumped to the brain. Now you are interested in the rate, rhythm, and quality of that pulse. Using the radial pulse, inside the wrist, where the thumb side of the hand joins the arm, is much more comfortable for the patient than pressing her neck. Press lightly with several fingertips.

RATE: The number of beats per minute. A range of 60-80 is normal in an adult. It will usually be higher in children, sometimes reaching a norm of 160 in an infant. Counting for one full minute is more accurate, but a count for 15 seconds and multiplying by four is acceptable and most often used. In the absence of a watch, take a pulse anyway. At least you can assess the rhythm and quality.

RHYTHM: There will be either a clock-like regularity or a sporadic irregularity.

QUALITY: This refers to the force exerted by the heart on each beat. The force will be best judged by its relation to previous pulse checks. A *normal* quality is strong, a *thready* pulse is weak and an indication of inadequate circulation, and a *bounding* pulse is abnormally forceful.

An absence of a radial pulse is cause for alarm. But delay panicking until you check the arm. The cause might be an injury to the arm or shoulder.

Respiration

Patients alerted to the fact that you're checking their respiration may voluntarily alter their breathing pattern. Keep your assessment a secret.

RATE: An adult normally breathes 12-20 times per minute. Children and infants breath faster.

RHYTHM: Normally, we breathe evenly and regularly, exhalations taking slightly longer than inhalations. Watch for shallowness or deepness, and irregularities in the pattern.

QUALITY: Normal breathing is quiet and effortless. Abnormal breathing might include labor, pain, noise (snores, wheezes, gurgles, gasps) and a flaring of the nostrils.

Skin

It's on the outside, away from the body's core where vital life processes are centered, but the skin gives pertinent information on the general well-being of our patient.

COLOR: Pink is the normal color of skin in the non-pigmented areas of the body—the lining of the eye, inside the mouth, fingernail beds. It may be difficult to detect subtle changes in darker complexions, but the overall color of the skin is also an indicator. The size of the blood vessels near the skin determines color. Vasodilation (widening vessels) produces a red, flushed color and indicates problems such as fever or hyperthermia. Vasoconstriction (narrowing vessels) produces pale or blotchy skin and may indicate shock or hypothermia. A blue hue, called cyanosis, shows a lack of oxygen. Yellowish skin tells of liver failure.

TEMPERATURE: The temperature of the skin can be significantly lower than the body's core and still be perfectly healthy. It will indicate, though, whether the patient is vasodilating and growing warmer, or vasoconstricting and getting cooler.

MOISTURE: Normal skin is relatively dry. Warmth and wetness from excessive sweating may be evident, but if the skin is cool and moist, it may indicate shock. Warm, dry skin may indicate dehydration.

Blood Pressure

A blood pressure reading is impossible to take without a device called a sphygmomanometer, and is more accurate if you have a stethoscope as well. It is mentioned briefly here because of its importance, along with a very crude field assessment technique.

Your beating heart creates pressure on the walls of your blood vessels. When the pressure drops too low for perfusion and adequate oxygenation to occur, tissues begin to die, and soon the organism follows. Blood pressure has two components: 1) the systolic pressure, measured when the heart is contracting, and 2) the diastolic, measured when the heart is at rest. A general norm is written as 120/80, but the pressure varies greatly from individual to individual.

As the pressure drops, skin becomes pale, then more and more cyanotic (bluish). The patient will become less coherent. Pulses begin to disappear. You'll lose the pulse in your feet first, then your wrist, and finally your neck. You can usually assume a patient with a strong radial pulse has a systolic BP of at least 90, high enough to sustain life. If you found the radial pulse of your patient earlier, and now it is gone, he is losing pressure and is at risk of dying.

The Medical History

As you practice, you will gain pride in your ability to perform a patient exam and take a set of vital signs. But the tricky part of assessment, and probably 80% of your final verdict, will come from information gathered as you interview your patient.

Approach with a calm, confident attitude, whether you feel it or not. An aura of calmness surrounding the scene will often do more for the sick and injured than all the splints and aspirin you can throw at them. Quietly say, "Hi, I read a book on backcountry medicine and I can help you." Don't scream: "What happened? What happened?"

If you haven't already, establish a relationship with your patient. It is more effective to say sincerely, "I know you must be afraid and in pain, but we'll make you as comfortable as possible," as opposed to panting, "You'll be okay. You'll be fine."

Always find a way to make your statements *positive*. Say: "Are you more comfortable sitting up or lying down?" rather than, "Which *hurts* more?"

Be enthusiastic without being a cheerleader. Be kind without being nauseating. Be honest without saying everything you're thinking. Beware of the tone of your voice. Beware of your patient's tendency to take the slightest offhand comment as truth. Discuss with your patients the possible plans of action. They have a right to their say in what happens.

A helpful mnemonic is SAMPLE:

SIGNS and SYPMTOMS: "Tell me about how you feel." (Pain, nausea, etc.)

ALLERGIES: "Are you allergic to anything you know of?"

MEDICATIONS: "Taking anything currently?" (Legal or illegal.) "Did you skip taking your medication?"

PAST HISTORY: "Is there anything possibly relevant I should know about your health?" Or, "Has anything like this happened before?" Or, "Are you seeing a doctor for anything?"

LAST MEAL: "When did you eat or drink last?"

EVENTS: "What led up to this?" And finally: "Is there anything else I should know?"

The questions you ask should not lead the patient on. Don't ask, "Is it a sharp pain?" Ask instead, "Can you describe the pain for me?"

If they are in pain or discomfort, another mnemonic is P Q R S T. What, if anything, PROVOKES the pain? What is the QUALITY of the pain? Does it RADIATE? Rate the SEVERITY. And what TIME did the problem start?

If patients are unconscious, you have to become even more of a Sherlock Holmes in your search for clues. Are they wearing *Medical Alert* tags on neck, wrists, ankles? Is there any information in their pockets? What can you learn from witnesses? From anyone around who knows them? What evidence does the scene hold for you? Seek answers to the A E I O U TIPS: Is their unconsciousness the result of Allergies, Epilepsy, Infection, Overdose, Underdose, Trauma, Insulin, Psychological, Stroke.

The SOAP Note

When time allows, or if there are spare hands at the scene, all the information gathered during assessment and what was done for treatment should be recorded on paper. You will never remember everything, vital signs slip away like autumn leaves in a high wind, and the patient deserves to have any physician who later takes over know the details of what happened and what was done. The note also becomes a legal record if a medical-legal question arises. Even if you're not sure what you're doing is absolutely correct, you want to record all your efforts in the patient's behalf. It shows you did your best.

The note can be divided into four sections for convenience of memory:
SUBJECTIVE: What happened to whom (include age, address and sex), where and when? What is the chief complaint?
OBJECTIVE: What did the physical exam reveal? What are the vital signs, and when did you do the following checks? What is the relevant medical history?
ASSESSMENT: What are the possible problems?
PLAN: What are you going to do?
Eventually you'll add to the note your name, the names of any other members of the aiding party and witnesses.

Sample SOAP Note

S: On (fill in date), (fill in name, address, sex) fell approximately 60 feet while rock climbing on Cannon Mountain, and pendulumed back-first into rock wall. Pt. was wearing no helmet. Pt. denies loss of consciousness. Pt. states: "Head hurts." Pain described as dull ache "like a bad headache" with no radiation. Pain described as constant "5" on scale of one to ten.

O: Exam revealed pain on palpation in back of head and upper chest toward backbone. No bruising or deformities noticed. Good circulation, sensation and motion noted in all four extremities. Vitals at 6PM were: LOC=A and oriented. Pulse=84, reg & strong. Breathing=14 & easy. Skin=pale and moist. No allergies. No meds. Last meal lunch at 12PM. Witness states: "He slipped while climbing."

A: Possible head and/or neck injury. Possible chest and/or spine injury.

P: Full head and spine immobilization in rigid litter. Evacuate. Monitor for changes.
    Addendum: 8PM:
        LOC=V. Pulse=60 & strong. Breathing=20 & labored.
        Skin=pale & moist. Speeded up evacuation.

The Barehanded Principles:

SECONDARY ASSESSMENT

1. Create an aura of calmness and confidence.
2. Do a complete head-to-toe physical examination.
3. Check (and keep checking) the vital signs: level of consciousness, pulse, respiration, skin.
4. Take a medical history.
5. Write a SOAP note.

Chapter 3
Shock

Our camp was set on the Muddy Boo after a long day of simmering in Old Town Trippers. It was Florida, it was August, it was hot, and it was humid. The canoes were cleaned and lashed to trees near the river. Dinner was over, and darkness settled over the camp like an electric blanket trained to kill.

Final instructions were given to the kids: "Don't leave your tents without your shoes. This is mean country, ready to take a bite out of you in many ways!" We were the last to zip up our doors against the descending horde of night marauders.

We called him Sugar Dog because he acted sweet but was ready to take a nip out of your backside if you turned. He left his tent deep in the night—without his shoes of course—when his brain lost an argument with his bladder over a question of urination. His half-muffled scream came from the darkness. No snakes, spiders, scorpions. No 'gators or wild pigs or rabid skunks. No broken glass or rusty shards of old cans. The Dog had thumped his big toe against a partially buried log.

The initial response to being injured is the same for all humans. A message runs from the site of the injury, in this case the big toe, to the brain. It is not an "ouch" message. It is an "alert" message, informing the brain something bad is happening. The brain throws the body into an alert status, preparing to deal with the problem. The heart rate speeds up and blood rushes out to the body faster. The respiratory rate increases, keeping the blood enriched with oxygen. The skin turns pale and clammy as the vessels near the edge of the body constrict to increase circulation to the vital inner organs. If you were watching Sugar Dog, your first indication something was wrong would be a change in his level of consciousness—he would appear anxious, a reflection of his brain's concern over the unknown extent of the injury.

With the vital processes secure, an unheard nerve "conversation" between the brain and the toe might be translated like this:

The brain says, "What's going on down there, toe?"

The toe says, "You stubbed me viciously. I'm probably broken!"

"That's it?" asks the brain. "Nothing life-threatening?"

"It seemed important to me," says the toe, now embarrassed over the commotion.

"What a wimp," mumbles the brain, and relaxes the alert status.

Sugar Dog looked relieved, his heart slowed down, he took a deep slow breath, his normal color returned. The toe, in one last act of defiance over the brain's control, started to throb as the nerve passageways returned to normal.

We found The Dog sitting on the ground, holding his toe and cursing. It only took a moment to assess him as relatively uninjured, and to begin our own cursing over his flagrant disregard for the rules.

If we had found a cause for real concern, let's say a deep gash in an artery of his lower leg, we would have had to handle the problem and the possibility of a serious sequel to the problem—shock.

Normal Physiology

Your cardiovascular system (heart, vessels and blood) is really two circulatory systems joined at the heart. The right side of the heart pumps blood to the lungs and back. The left side pushes oxygen-rich blood to all parts of the body and back. Both circuits work simultaneously. Cardiac output, the amount of blood pumped out by the heart every minute, is normally enough to meet the needs of all the cells of your body.

Blood leaves the heart through arteries that branch and narrow to arterioles that branch and narrow to capillaries. At the capillaries, the oxygen (and nutrients picked up from the digestive system) are diffused across cell walls, exchanged for carbon dioxide and the waste products of metabolism. The waste-carrying blood moves out the other end of the capillaries into venules that come together to form veins. The veins return blood to the heart. Veins are more numerous than arteries and can hold more of your blood. There is less pressure in the veins, and they have little one-way doors to keep the blood from backing up. All vessels can dilate or constrict to meet varying demands from the body. Your body's systems are designed to support the lives of your cells. When cellular life cannot be maintained, death of the organism occurs. The constant bathing of cells with life-sustaining fluid under proper pressure is called perfusion.

Shock

Shock is an inadequate perfusion of the body's cells with oxygenated blood. It results when cardiac output is too low to keep the cells washed with enough blood under enough pressure to allow diffusion to take place. Shock can be caused by failure of one or more of the three parts of the cardiovascular system.

1) HYPOVOLEMIC SHOCK is a result of loss of fluid from the system. It can be produced by external or internal blood loss, plasma loss from burns, or dehydration from diarrhea, vomiting and excessive sweating.

2) CARDIOGENIC SHOCK is a result of "pump failure" leading to a decrease in blood flow and a fall in blood pressure.

3) VASOGENIC SHOCK results when the resistance of the muscular vessel walls relax and blood pools in the veins, returning to the heart at an inadequate level. This can come from damage to the central nervous system (e.g. spinal cord damage), body-wide infection, or a severe allergic reaction.

Shock is a progressive problem, passing through three stages on its way to causing death.

1) During the COMPENSATORY STAGE, the body compensates for the damage by increasing its activity level.

2) The PROGRESSIVE (DECOMPENSATORY) STAGE begins when the compensatory mechanisms fail, and the condition of the patient declines, often rapidly.

3) The IRREVERSIBLE STAGE is reached when inadequate perfusion results in the cells of vital organs starting to die, when even the most definitive measures may not save the patient.

Whatever the cause, shock victims share similar signs and symptoms, all deriving from inadequate perfusion. Their level of consciousness is one of *anxiety* and *restlessness*, progressing to unconsciousness and coma. Their *heart rate increases*, and often feels weak and thready. *Abnormal respirations*, usually quick and shallow, progress to labored. Victims *sweat* heavily, the skin feeling *cool and clammy*, and progressively becoming cyanotic or ashen gray in color. They often complain of *thirst* from dehydration and *nausea* from inadequate perfusion of the stomach. The progressive stage will lead to *dull eyes* and a *blood pressure drop*.

The severity of shock is relative to the extent of the injury and whether or not the cause can be treated. For the patient to be treated successfully in the backcountry, early recognition and management are essential!

MAXIM:

ASSUME SHOCK IN ALL PATIENTS WITH INJURY OR ILLNESS

Treatment of Shock

The primary goal in the treatment of shock is the same as with any patient—secure and maintain an airway. If there is a cause that can be treated (as in direct pressure on severe bleeding), do it. Since your patient is suffering from an insufficiency of oxygen, it would be wonderful if you could give supplemental oxygen, but that is most often not possible in the wilderness. It is very important to keep patients calm and reassured! Have them lie down, if they aren't already, and elevate their feet about a foot if the elevation does not aggravate an injury. Elevation of the legs can be achieved by having patients lie down on a slope with their feet slightly uphill. Elevation increases blood flow to the vital organs. Keep them warm. Anticipate the worst, and begin immediate plans for evacuation to a medical facility. Patients with progressive shock need a physician's intervention.

MAXIM:

PATIENTS IMPROVING CAN STAY. PATIENTS GETTING WORSE MUST GO.

Unless the evacuation is very long, do not give the patient anything to eat or drink. The possibility of vomiting is high and dangerous. Small amounts of food and especially water might necessarily be given over a long evacuation, if the patient is alert and able to accept a cup and drink from it.

Figure 3-1
Shock treatment position.

The Barehanded Principles:
SHOCK

1) Assume shock until proven otherwise.

2) Maintain an adequate airway.

3) Treat the cause if possible.

4) Keep the patient calm and reassured.

5) Keep the patient lying down with feet elevated.

6) Keep the patient warm.

7) Do not give food and water unless necessary, and only if the patient is alert.

8) Monitor the patient closely for changes.

9) Plan an immediate evacuation if the patient is not compensating.

Chapter 4
Spinal Cord Injury Management

Murray and I are making our way down the steep slope of Denali Pass. Stretched below us on the snow are two victims, one stirring, the other motionless. Our intention was to summit on this unusually clear Alaskan day. We saw the two climbers ahead of us fall, tumbling 600 feet, head-over-heels. One pack flew off. An ice axe, glinting in the afternoon sunlight, arched through the air. Unfortunately, it was still attached to the climber's wrist.

There is blood on the snow, leaking from where the axe cut a hole in the face of the unconscious victim. He is breathing rapidly with grunting moans on exhalation. Primary surveys reveal the other is likely to have suffered no serious injury, but the unconscious moaner reacts to pain in his head and neck. It is the kind of scenario you hate most—a possible cervical spine injury deep in the wilderness.

The human spine is a marvelously intricate structure of 33 bones (vertebrae) that give support yet flexibility to the body. By restricting motion to within definite bounds, the bones provide protection for the delicate spinal cord, the super-highway of nerves running down the center of the vertebrae.

The top seven bones of the spine work with the muscles of the neck to support the head. These cervical vertebrae are the smallest and most flexible in the spinal column, and, as you might expect, are the most susceptible to serious injury. Next, 12 thoracic vertebrae have ribs attached to them, helping to form the chest cavity that holds the heart and lungs. The lower back is composed of five vertebrae, the largest components of the spine. Since the last two thoracic vertebrae are attached to ribs that float freely in front (not being attached to the sternum), that region of the spine (T-10 to L-1) gives us more rotational freedom, and consequently is another high risk area for injury. Below the lumbar spine a lump of bones called the sacrum holds on to the pelvis. Finally the little coccyx reminds us, perhaps, that we once extended farther in that direction. The fused bones of the sacrum and coccyx gives us the total of 33. The spinal cord becomes loosely connected strings of nerves, like a horse's tail, in the lumbar region, and ends before the sacrum.

Types of Spinal Injuries

1) *The Uninterrupted Spinal Cord*: There may be broken vertebrae, or there may not. There may be torn supporting ligaments in the spine. But the cord itself is not damaged. The patient needs to be carefully handled to insure the cord remains uninterrupted.

2) *The Partial Spinal Cord Injury*: There are probably fractures and definitely swelling that interrupts the blood supply to the cord. The result is loss of some motor function in the arms and/or legs, some loss of feeling, and some weakness. A partial injury can progress to a full one.

3) *The Full Spinal Cord Injury*: There is a severe interruption of spinal cord function.

Assessing the Injury

1) Any mechanism forcing the spine out of its normal range of motion or overloading it beyond its ability to bear weight can cause a serious injury. Of specific concern are violent flexion motions (especially chin to chest), violent rotations, and loads that compress the spine. Accidents commonly providing this type of violence in the backcountry are falls from a height and diving injuries. Even when the faller lands on his feet, the spine can compress excessively, and certainly if he lands in a sitting position. A diver who hits a submerged object, or even one who hits the water wrong, can overload and over-flex his spine. Excessive flexion can occur when a skier hits a tree at high speed. A less common but devastating spinal injury called a distraction (the opposite of compression) is possible when a climber falls and momentarily dangles from a rope or rack. And, of course, a combination of factors may be at work in the accident.

2) Assessing a patient thoroughly includes gathering information about the forces, movement and materials involved in the traumatic event. These insights become even more significant when evaluating a

possible spinal injury. Some victims with seriously injured spines will get up and walk, not complaining of pain or loss of movement until permanent paralysis sets in. Your job as a rescuer is to recognize the chance of an injury and treat the patient accordingly.

3) In the patient exam, check carefully for pain and tenderness in the neck. Be aware that distracting injuries (e.g. broken bones, bleeding wounds) may make it difficult for the patient to focus on relatively mild spinal pain.

4) Include a thorough neurological checkup in your secondary check for motion: Ask patients to wiggle their toes, and have them press against your hand with their feet as against the accelerator of a car, and then the opposite motion, lifting their feet against pressure from your hand. Check for sensation: Can they feel you touching their feet and hands? Check for circulation: Do they have palpable pulses or at least capillary refill in their fingers and toes? Spinal cord injury can be indicated by one or more of these things.

Checklist of warning signs of spinal cord injury:

1) A sufficient mechanism of injury.

2) Pain and/or tenderness in the spine.

3) Altered sensations in the extremities (tingling, numbness, weakness, loss of ability to move, complaints of cold or heat).

4) Beware of distracting injuries which may mask spinal pain and tenderness.

Managing the Spinal Injury

The goal is to prevent any further injury, and to do it the neck and spinal cord need to be immobilized and stabilized. Your immediate care should include telling your patient to lie still! An extra set of hands immobilizing the patient's head is very useful. Whether the patient is lying, sitting or standing, someone should move to their rear and take gentle but firm control of the neck by holding on to the head.

But what if the scene isn't safe? What if an avalanche is pouring down the mountainside? What if they're lying half in an icy cold stream? Getting patients to a safe place must take precedence over injury to their spine, but not at the exclusion of the spine. The answer is Body Elevation And Movement (BEAM). Get as many hands on the patient as possible, with the firm ones still on the head. At the command of the head-immobilizer, lift the patient as a unit and BEAM him to a safe place without moving the spine from the position you found it in.

If the patient lies unconscious, you must first assume a neck injury until it is proven otherwise. If the neck lies at an odd angle, it should be carefully straightened before treatment is continued. This can be accomplished safely with slow, gentle motion. Move the neck to the neutral position, the spine in a line. STOP if the movement appears to cause the patient pain. STOP if you meet resistance.

Patients on their side can be log-rolled on to their back before treatment is continued. Manual stabilization should be applied to the neck during movement, and at all times until the head is immobilized by some mechanical means (e.g. backboard). Of course, a log-roll can move patients to their side if a pad must be put under them to keep the cold ground from eating their body heat. With the pad in place, roll them back on to it. (If your group is small, the pad can be used as a sled for moving the patient to a safer, more comfortable place.)

Figure 4-1
Log-rolling a patient.

With the spine in the neutral position, the next step is to stabilize the cervical spine in place. Ambulances carry a cervical collar, a device that wraps around the neck to prevent excessive movement, especially the deadly chin-to-chest flexion. In the backcountry, extra clothing can be wrapped carefully around the patient's neck. Better yet, cut the end of a foamlite sleeping pad to fit the patient's neck and tie or tape it in place. A commercially-made SAM Splint can be formed into a cervical collar.

Figure 4-2
Manual stabilization of a possible neck injury.
(Inset: cervical collar)

Do not be deceived into thinking the collar is adequate stabilization. Manual, hands-on attention to the neck must still be maintained until the whole body of the patient can be immobilized on a rigid support. This rigid support takes the form of a full backboard in an ambulance. In the wilds, you are probably looking at a long wait for someone to go for help. Your patient needs to be made Free Of Any Movement (FOAM) in an inflexible litter. FOAMing is very difficult to accomplish with an improvised litter. It has been done by lashing external pack frames together with great attention to detail, and lashing dry limbs from the forest floor together with even greater attention to detail. (Green limbs flex too much!) In winter, skis may possibly be used to construct a rigid sled for the transportation of a spinal injury.

Once a litter is available, it is critical to FOAM the body of the patient in place (lots of padding and many straps) before tying down the head. A sudden movement of the patient, with the head tied down and the body not, can cause all you've been trying so hard to prevent. The body straps should include the shoulders. They work best if the straps crisscross the patient's chest, putting less strain on the diaphragm while holding the torso securely down. The head should be padded and tied or taped to the litter.

As with any patient, but certainly with this one, you need to keep calm communication going with this person you're lashing to a rack of torture. Look for places the rope, or tubular webbing, or whatever you're using, may be biting into the patient, and pad there. Pad in places the rigid support may produce painful pressure, like behind the knees and under the small of the back.

Proceed with great care. Permanent spinal injuries are often the result of improper handling on the scene. The spinal patient should be given consideration as a helicopter evacuation, if a chopper is available.

Clearing the Spine

If the patient has had an accident that could cause spinal cord injury, yet there are no immediate signs and symptoms of injury, treat for spinal cord injury anyway. But, if after a minimum of two hours, no signs and symptoms have developed, you may, deep in the backcountry, allow the patient to move slowly and carefully. If slow, careful movement produces no signs or symptoms (pain, tingling, numbness, weakness), greater movement may be allowed. If at any time signs develop, re-treat for the possibility of a spinal cord injury.

The Barehanded Principles:
SPINAL CORD INJURY MANAGEMENT

1) *Secure the scene*, by BEAMing the patient if necessary.

2) *Secure the airway*, by slow, careful movement of the head if necessary. Open the airway with a jaw-thrust instead of a head-tilt chin-lift if necessary.

3) Improvise a *cervical collar*.

4) Keep hands-on maintenance to prevent uncontrolled movement of the spine.

5) Go for (or in desperation, improvise) a rigid litter.

6) FOAM the patient on the litter for careful evacuation.

7) Remember, once stabilized, a spinal injury is not an immediate threat to life. Don't rush and kill somebody.

Chapter 5
Wound Management & Infection

Even in July the Wind River Mountains are a chilly place. It was a classic, cold Rocky Mountain morning that found David and Bobby standing at the base of the Southwest Ridge of Nylon Peak, near the Continental Divide. By the time David began to inch his way up the initial pitch, his hands were truly numb. At some point along the rope length, cold flesh overgripped sharp granite. As the angle eased, David shook his hands for warmth and felt his own blood slap against his cheek. This was the first he knew of the damage to his fingers. He arrived at the belay with a left hand covered in blood, displaying at least six magnificent flaps of avulsed skin, two each on the pinky, ring and middle fingers.

Once off the climb, Bobby trimmed the ragged, dead tissue, leaving six open wounds. Lots of soap and water left him satisfied, and David grimacing. David spent 10 days on a daily routine of re-cleaning and re-bandaging. He hiked with the hand bandaged and inside a nylon overmitt. By the end of the trip he had some dry scabs, some new pink skin, and was well on his way to being able to make a fist again.

Our skin does a lot of great things for us. It is essential in regulating the inner temperature of our bodies, which must be carefully controlled for us to stay alive. It oils itself to maintain flexibility so we don't dry out and split open. It provides a sensory avenue, allowing us to intimately contact the world around us. But we are concerned here with the skin as a waterproof layer, keeping inside fluid in and outside fluid out, and the skin as protection against a wide world of bacteria waiting vigilantly to invade us.

You'd think Mother Nature, in all her infinite wisdom, would have made us tougher on the outside where the wear and tear takes place. Not so! We are forever abusing our skin with bashes, scrapes, nicks, slices and impalements, opening our defenses to blood loss and any germ that happens to be crawling past. Knowing how to manage injuries to skin and the underlying layers of fat and muscle is a significant part of providing adequate backcountry care.

Wound Management

Any disruption in the vasculature of our bodies results in a bleeding wound. The immediate severity of the injury depends on the number of vessels we disrupt, and whether they are spurting arteries, flowing veins or oozing capillaries. Sometimes the damage is internal (a bruise, a sprain, a broken bone) and the bleeding is characterized by swelling and discoloration. Sometimes the damage is external and characterized by blood running out and making a mess.

Our natural response to being opened in unnatural places is a remarkable and involuntary attempt to return to a balanced internal state. There is a prompt constriction of the tissue around the wound, compressing the small vessels and slowing blood loss. For 10 minutes or so the vasculature of our entire body will constrict, reducing blood loss even more. Attracted to the site of the injury, the platelets in our blood form plugs in the torn vessels. A process called coagulation builds a clot of elastic protein filaments restoring the integrity of the vasculature until full healing occurs. It is a wonderful thing that even small furry mammals can do.

You, as a rescuer, want to have three goals in managing a wound:

1) Stop the bleeding.

2) Prevent infection.

3) Promote healing.

NOTE: Wear protective gloves when touching blood or other body fluids. Wash your hands thoroughly after removing gloves.

Stop the Bleeding

Almost all bleeding can be stopped with direct pressure and elevation. Apply the pressure with your gloved hand directly on the site of the injury, and elevate the wound above the patient's heart. Sometimes it is necessary to remove or cut away clothing to get a good look at the injured area. It is best to get a sterile dressing from your first-aid kit to place on the wound before applying pressure, but if the bleeding is serious, jump in right away with gloved hand, a wadded bandana or T-shirt, and a desire to stop the blood loss. If the bleeding is slow, it is perfectly okay to let it go for a few minutes, which actually cleans out the wound a bit. Keep the patient in a restful position, and avoid any unnecessary movement for at least the time it takes for the natural plug to form.

Direct pressure and elevation are contraindicated in places where the injury could be made worse by those actions. These places include:

1) A patient's neck, near the trachea, where you might cut off the air supply. Neck bleeds can usually be stopped by pinching carefully around the opening with your fingers.

2) A patient's skull, where you might push cracked bone into the brain. Open head wounds tend to bleed ferociously because the vessels in the scalp don't spasm and seal themselves off as they do in thinner-skinned areas of the body. If there is a suspicion of skull fracture, place bulky sterile dressings over the wound and apply light pressure. When that doesn't work, pull the edges of the wound together and tape it closed. Bandages designed for holding wound edges together work best, but any tape might do.

Prevent Infection (Wound Cleaning)

The prevention of infection almost equates with proper wound cleaning. A healthy cleaning also speeds healing and reduces scarring. The basic techniques include scrubbing, irrigation and debridement.

Start by carefully washing your own hands and putting on protective gloves. Avoid breathing into, coughing around, or drooling all over an open wound.

Scrubbing is to clean thoroughly around the wound. You can use an antiseptic preparation created for wound cleaning (providone-iodine, benzalkonium chloride, hexachlorophene), but soap and clean water will work. Scrub with a sterile gauze pad away from the open injury. Scrubbing can be used directly on the surface of an abrasion if foreign material is embedded there (see below). Finally, rinse out anything that falls into the wound, including the antiseptic preparation created for wound cleaning. Anything left in the wound retards healing.

The purpose of irrigation is to remove contaminants from the wound surface. A high pressure stream of an acceptable solution is directed into the opening. Optimally, you would use a syringe and needle, or an irrigation syringe. You can use any sort of clean plastic bag with a pinhole punched in it, or melt a pinhole in the top of a standard water bottle. Hold the irrigation device two to four inches above the wound and perpendicular to the wound, and drive the solution (or clean water) forcefully into the wound. Keep the wound tipped so the solution runs out. Use at least a half-liter of solution to irrigate a moderate-sized wound.

And finish with a final rinse of disinfected water.

Debridement is the removal of visualized foreign particles and dead tissue. Any foreign matter that does not come out with irrigation can be picked out with discrimination and tweezers you have sterilized in boiling water or soaked in povidone-iodine solution. A guideline for dead tissue removal is: Trimming dead tissue causes no pain. Most removal of dead tissue should wait until it's deemed necessary.

Specific Wounds

BRUISES: Or contusions, as the erudite like to call them, are pockets of blood collecting in soft tissue after a blow or a tearing motion (as in twisting a joint too far). Blood seeping from torn vessels produce the color, and the pain and swelling are relative to the severity of the injury. Bruises are an example of a closed wound, one not open to the outside world.

Bruises are usually minor, but a big bruise can be treated with an application of RICE (Rest, Ice, Compression, Elevation). After about 48 hours, heat can be applied to stimulate healthy circulation. Beware: Bruises will freeze sooner than normal tissue in extremes of cold.

ABRASIONS: A piece of skin has been rubbed or scraped away, leaving a weeping raw spot that hurts a lot. The pain can be very bothersome because nerve endings (those receptors responsible for the "ouch" of an injury) are near the surface and not buried in fat or muscle. This type of wound is often dirty.

Convince the patient of the efficacy of letting you scrub the area clean. Anesthetic cleansing pads provide some reduction in the pain that often accompanies scrubbing an abrasion. If you choose to carry a surgical scrub brush in your first-aid kit, it will make cleaning easier. Soap and water will work just fine. Follow scrubbing with a thorough rinse with clean water. Keeping the wound slightly moist will reduce healing time and scarring. To do this, apply a thin coat of antibiotic ointment, or use a microthin film dressing. If you use ointment, cover the wound with sterile gauze. Scabs work, but they don't work as well as ointment or specialized dressings.

LACERATIONS: The skin has been opened in either a neat or ragged line. After the bleeding has stopped and the wound is clean, it might gape open. You will have less bother with it (and it'll heal faster) if you pull it closed with wound closure strips. A bead of tincture of benzoin compound along both sides of the laceration will make the closure strips stick better. Stick the end of a closure strip on one side of the wound, and one on the other, and use the strips as little handles to approximate the edges of the laceration. Do NOT pull it tightly closed. Without wound closure strips, you can use butterfly adhesive bandages or tape. If you pull a laceration closed, you must watch it closely for signs of infection. It is easy to trap germs in a closed wound outside a sterile hospital environment. They like it in there. They want to be kept moist and warm where they grow best. Cover the wound with sterile gauze or a micro-thin film dressing.

Large dirty wounds and wounds inflicted by animal bites should not be closed. Cover them with sterile gauze, leaving an antiseptic soaked piece of gauze in the wound to keep the drainage process going while you evacuate the patient.

Consider seeing a doctor for all gaping wounds, large or small, to be checked for underlying damage, and infection, and for stitches to reduce scarring, especially lacerations of the face and lacerations over joints.

AVULSIONS: Something has sliced in at an angle, leaving a flap of flesh that lifts partially away from the rest of the body. If possible, replace the flap before applying direct pressure. Lift the flap to irrigate well underneath, and after cleaning, this little "trapdoor" should be bandaged back in as close to its original position as possible. The wound will be less sensitive, and the avulsed piece might grow back into place. If the avulsed part is hopelessly de-circulated, it will die. If it is small and ratty, sometimes trimming off the ragged ends is okay before bandaging. Otherwise, wait to see if the piece survives before hacking away at it.

AMPUTATIONS: Sometimes the avulsed part is totally separated from the body at the time of the injury. Even small parts, like the tip of a finger, can often be replaced successfully in the emergency room, often several hours after the accident. The salvage process requires the proper handling of the amputated part. It needs to be kept moist and cold, but not wet and frozen. For the backcountry, the technique most likely to work would be wrapping the part in slightly moist sterile gauze, putting the gauze in a sealable plastic bag, and putting the bag in ice water. Any combination of the above is better than letting it dry out unwrapped or swell up from being too wet. Even if you have no hope for the amputated piece of person, packing it out will be an act of kindness and environmental sensitivity.

PUNCTURES: Human skin, being elastic, immediately closes around whatever gets stuck into it, effectively wiping off and sealing in a load of germs and dirt when the puncturing object pulls out. If you get there soon enough, irrigating a small puncture wound, encouraging it to bleed, is okay. Scrub the area and squirt an iodine solution as deeply into the hole as possible, attempting to attack the embedded bacteria. Without iodine, irrigate the wound with water, at least a liter of it. Do not close the wound with tape or a tight bandage. The wound needs to drain. A large puncture wound can have a piece of sterile gauze left in it for a couple of days to hold it open in order to encourage draining.

Puncture wounds can be insidious, a minor wound on the surface with major damage hidden below. A look at the offending object and a knowledge of the underlying anatomy can be very useful in determining the extent of the injury.

Any serious puncture wound should be watched carefully for signs of infection, and considered for an immediate evacuation.

IMPALED OBJECTS: It is unique to find a puncturing object still stuck into a human. Most people usually pull it out as an instinctive reaction. And so you end up treating a puncture wound. But the object may still be there because it broke off too short to grab, or it is embedded too deeply, or the shape of the object caused it to catch inside the flesh.

If the object is large and you can get to a medical facility with relative ease, the object is probably best padded to prevent movement, and the patient carried out of the woods. In many cases there is nothing easy about getting to help. You can't heal with something stuck in you, you can't prevent infection, and you aren't happy.

Figure 5-1
Stabilization of an impaled object.

Removal of impaled objects in the backcountry is an oft-debated subject. Yanking on an object can stimulate serious bleeding and damage underlying structures. But impaled objects sometimes make evacuation very difficult. They can be impossible to stabilize over rough terrain. Metal, like an ice axe, can suck a significant amount of heat out of a cold patient.

If the object is through a cheek, or in any other way endangering the patient's airway, there is ample agreement on removing it carefully. If the object is loosely embedded, removal is simple and beneficial to you and the patient. If the object is in an extremity, removal is probably safe. Note the object's shape and angle of entry, and remove accordingly.

If the impaled object is large, and in a body cavity (chest or abdomen), it is usually best to stabilize it in place as snugly as possible, and evacuate with speed and great care.

There are no great answers here, but there are sound reasons for removing an impaled object in the backcountry if the situation warrants.

Promote Healing (Dressings & Bandages)

The dressing is the primary covering of an open wound. It protects, reduces pain, absorbs exudates, and gives psychological relief. It should be sterile, non-adherent, porous, resistant to bacterial infiltration and easy to use. Avoid confusion by purchasing a few pre-packaged dressings from your local drugstore. Buy an assortment of gauze pads, sponges, bandages, and micro-thin film dressings. If a sterile dressing is unavailable, a piece of cloth can be sterilized by boiling. The formula for sterilization is a rolling boil for five minutes plus one minute more for every 1,000 feet above sea level you are. This formula, once again, sterilizes, and should not be confused with disinfection, a simpler process. (Of course, for minor open wounds, disinfection, just bringing the water to a rolling boil, might be enough. Consider the severity of the wound, and the time it will take to reach medical aid.)

Do not touch the sterile dressing except on the edges where it will not contact the wound. To provide adequate protection, the dressing should extend at least one inch past the borders of the wound.

The function of the bandage is to fix, protect, and further assist the dressing. It can be strips of clean cotton, elastic wraps, roller gauze, tape, or improvised out of anything you have. The usefulness of a bandage is handicapped by being too loose, and dangerous if applied tightly enough to restrict circulation. It should be put on snugly, and checked often. Do not hide rings or anything that can cut off healthy blood flow if swelling occurs. If tape is used, it should be well away from the opening to keep the sticky stuff (adhesive) out of the wound. Tape should be wrapped loosely around an extremity, to prevent turning it into a tourniquet.

Tincture of benzoin compound applied to skin before taping makes the tape stick better for more long lasting results. Keep the benzoin out of the wound. It encourages infection, and it hurts!

Specific Dressings & Bandages

ADHESIVE TAPE: Several widths are available. One-inch wide is a fine choice for the backcountry. Two-inch wide can be torn easily into a one-inch width if needed.

ADHESIVE BANDAGE STRIPS: These self-adhering strips combine a dressing and a bandage (e.g. Band-Aids). They come in various sizes—

one inch by three inches usually doing the job—and are great for minor open wounds. Special shapes for knuckles and fingertips can be purchased.

ELASTIC WRAPS: Although mostly used to support sprained joints, these wraps (e.g. Ace) can compress a large wound while holding the dressing in place.

GAUZE PADS: These sterile pads start as small as one inch by one inch and go on to huge dimensions. Four by fours work most of the time.

MICRO-THIN FILM DRESSINGS: See-through and water-resistant, they let air pass through while retaining healthy moisture near the wound. You can monitor a wound without removing the dressing.

NON-ADHESIVE DRESSINGS: Special inner surface discourages this dressing from sticking to a wound.

ROLL GAUZE: These rolls of gauze conform to the shape of the body. They come in many sizes, but four inches wide will work in most cases.

TRIANGULAR BANDAGES: As the name implies, these are triangles of cloth. They can be created out of large bandanas with a simple fold. They can be used to tie on dressings, working well in difficult places like on the head. If large enough, they can be used as slings and swathes for the arm.

WOUND CLOSURE STRIPS: These allow neat closure of gaping wounds. They can be improvised from tape. Special bandages (e.g. butterflies) can be used to close wounds.

The Barehanded Principles:

WOUND MANAGEMENT
1. Take a close look at the injury.
2. Wash your hands, wear gloves, wash your hands again.
3. Control the bleeding, if necessary, with direct pressure and elevation.
4. Clean the wound thoroughly.
5. Dress and bandage the wound.
6. Splint the severely wounded extremity.
7. Watch for signs of infection.

Infection

On a worldwide basis, infection, the multiplication of harmful micro-organisms in tissues of the body, is still a leading cause of death. In America we have become more civilized, and we die most often from the peaceful and sedentary problem of heart disease. We remain covered with microscopic life forms, especially on our skin, and in our mouths, throats and intestines. Most of these organisms are harmless. If our internal defenses against disease are down, and if an injury breaks us open, and if we contact a lot of harmful organisms, we might still develop a dangerous infection.

As a wound heals, an unseen barrier develops on the inside of the body, sealing off the wounded area. White blood cells attack entrenched germs that have worked their way inside. Much of the contamination that migrates to the surface and drains out as white or faintly yellow pus is WBC's that died in the line of duty.

Some of the contamination is dumped internally into the lymphatic system and carried to lymph nodes where it is picked up by our circulatory system and eventually cleaned out of the blood and excreted from our body. The wound wonderfully maintains itself. This complex body process is called inflammation. It looks a little red and swollen, feels a little warm and tender.

If the bacteria trapped in a wound are too abundant for the inflammation process to handle, infection will occur. The redness becomes redder, the warmth becomes heat, the swelling swells, and tissue begins to harden past the borders of the wound. These signs usually show up in 24-48 hours, but they can develop days after the accident. The pain may become great, and mobility of an extremity may be limited.

Wounds on the hand commonly become infected. Hands get less healthy circulation, and are the most likely place for us to cut ourselves.

As infection spreads, lymph nodes can grow large and painful as they attempt to catch and kill the contamination, a condition known as lymphadentitis. The principal nodes are located in the elbows and knees, neck, groin and along the mid-to-lower backbone. Less common in infected wounds, lymphangitis produces the red streaks that sometimes appear just under the skin. The streaks move from the wound toward the nearest lymph node as lymphatic vessels become inflamed. Should the infection reach the bloodstream, the result will likely be septicemia, sometimes called "blood poisoning," and the possibility of life-threatening shock (see *Shock*).

Some wounds are more susceptible to infection than others. Be especially careful of flesh torn open by the teeth of animals, the bites of cats and humans being especially prone to infection. Infection is likely to result from crushing injuries, burns that open the skin, and severe frostbite. Heavy foreign body contamination is responsible for a lot of problems, as with an unnoticed splinter of wood buried in a foot or hand.

Any infection, whatever the source, produces similar signs and symptoms once it spreads throughout a patient's system. The victim develops a fever with accompanying chills and malaise. Serious infections often cause headache, nausea, vomiting or back pain.

Precious few places on Earth are far from an antibiotic, but way out in the backcountry an infection might become a serious threat to life. *Note: When traveling days from medical assistance, consider asking your physician for a prescription antibiotic and written guidelines for its use.* Gas gangrene, for instance, the result of an anaerobic bacterium that produces rapidly spreading tissue destruction, can cause death in as little as 30 hours. Gangrenous wounds stir up an abundance of dark, foul-smelling pus.

If you suspect serious infection, evacuate your patient to a medical facility as soon as possible. In the meantime, provide rest, warmth, a soft or liquid diet, and a high fluid intake. Aspirin, acetaminophen or ibuprofen may be given to reduce the fever. Stronger pain killers, if you have them, can temporarily ease the suffering. As you head for a doctor, keep track of the medications given. And keep tabs on the patient's temperature, if you have a thermometer.

You can aid your patient's struggle against an infected wound by opening the injury and cleaning it thoroughly. Soaking the wound in salty water as hot as the injured person can tolerate can be very helpful in the cleaning process. Hot compresses may also stimulate the wound to drain.

> NOTE: For more advanced methods of wilderness wound management, refer to *Wilderness Medicine*, Fourth Edition, by William Forgey, M.D., ICS Books, Incorporated, Merrillville, Indiana (800) 541-7323.

The Barehanded Principles:

INFECTION

1. Watch for a wound with increasing redness, swelling, pain and pus.

2. Watch for fever, malaise and red streaks just under the skin.

3. Soak and clean the wound thoroughly.

4. As much as possible keep the patient rested and warm, with a soft diet and high fluid intake.

5. If available, give medications for fever, pain and infection.

6. Evacuate.

Chapter 6
Burns

A burn, although common, is seldom a serious backcountry injury. They can be a nuisance, and they can lead to more significant problems if improperly treated. On occasion a burn can produce a life-threat.

Some chemicals, strong acids or alkalis mostly, can burn skin, but they are rarely carried beyond the roadhead. Electricity, in the form of lightning, is a potential hazard. A lightning strike usually gives us much more to be concerned about than the burns it might leave on our patient. Radiation from the sun is a very common cause of minor outdoor burning. But a thermal burn is the one that will most likely involve you, a burn produced by an extreme of temperature.

With any burn, there are three criteria determining the severity of the injury: depth, extent and location.

Depth

First-degree burns are superficial in depth, and do little to disrupt human tissue. The skin is irritated, red, painful. They rarely produce a need for an evacuation. Cool compresses and moisturizing lotions make the patient feel better.

Second-degree burns destroy some tissue. They are partial thickness burns, producing blisters that form minutes to hours after the initial contact with heat. If they are extensive, over more than 15% of the body's surface, they may become a threat to life (see below). With a moderate amount of second-degree burning, the patient's level of pain and discomfort will help you decide how fast to evacuate.

Third-degree burns extend through the full thickness of the skin, leaving charred remains of tissue (or blanched skin if the mechanism was scalding). It is popular to point out the lack of pain in third-degree burns due to the destruction of nerve endings in the skin, but the site is usually surrounded by second- and first-degree injuries that cause pain. Almost all third-degree burns deserve evacuation, but unless the burn covers around 15% of the body surface, shock and death seldom occur.

Extent

The extent or size of a burn is important. In adults the *Rule of Nines* can be applied to aid in determining the extent. The Rule says the head and neck are about 9% of the surface of a human, the arms are 9% each, legs are 18% each, the back of the torso is 18%, and the front of the torso is another 18%. The missing 1% is found on the genitals. In infants and small children, the head is a significantly larger percentage of their body surface. Consider the head of infants to be 18% of their surface, the legs 13% to 14% each.

Figure 6-1
Rule of Nines.

For smaller areas, the *Rule of Palm Surface* can be used. This rule calls the area covered by your patient's hand approximately one percent of the total surface area of that person's body.

Location

The location of the burn will help determine its severity. A burn injury to respiratory tract, if it causes difficulty breathing, can become a threat to life. Watch for hoarseness, a brassy cough, or a cough producing sooty sputum, or any combination of the above. Look for burns on the face and scorched facial hair. These people need to be rushed out to a hospital. Burns to the hands, feet and genitals can cause critical loss of function.

Initial Care of the Patient

Emergency care of burn patients is initially the same despite the severity of the injury: Stop The Burning Process. If they are in flames, smother the flames. Immediately flood the burned area in cold, clean water by pouring it on, by immersion, or by covering the area with a soaking wet, clean piece of cloth. Take off any burned clothing and anything constricting in the area of the burn (rings, bracelets, watches)—but do not try to remove melted plastic that sticks to the skin. It is important to remember that hot skin and underlying tissues will continue to burn even after the source of the heat has been removed. Keep up the flood of water for at least 10 minutes.

Keep the patient warm. Keep the injured body parts elevated. Encourage the patient to drink as much fluid, especially water, as he or she will tolerate.

Treatment for the Burn

Once the burning process has been stopped, caring for the burn itself is often the least important aspect of burn management. All burn wounds are sterile for 24-48 hours. Burn management is aimed primarily at keeping the wound clean and reducing pain.

1. Gently wash the wound with slightly warm water and mild soap. Pat dry. Remove the skin from blisters that have popped open (but do not open blisters).

2. Dress the burn with a thin layer of antibiotic ointment.

3. Cover the burn with a gauze pad or a thin layer of roll gauze, or apply clean dry clothing. Covering wounds reduces pain and evaporative losses, but do not use an occlusive dressing (one that lets no air or water through).

4. When evacuation is imminent, do not re-dress or re-examine the injury. But if evacuation is distant, re-dress twice a day by removing old dressings, re-washing (and removing the old ointment), and putting on fresh ointment and a fresh, clean, dry covering. (Note: You may have to soak off the old dressing with clean, tepid water.)

5. Do NOT use ice on a burn. Do NOT leave wet packs on burns for very long.

6. Keep burned extremities elevated to minimize swelling. Swelling retards healing and encourages infection.

7. For burn pain (including sunburn), ibuprofen is probably the best over-the-counter medication.

8. If you have no ointment, no dressings, and/or no confidence, leave the burn alone. Burn surfaces dry into a scab-like covering which, although not the best treatment, will provide a significant amount of protection.

The Barehanded Principles:
BURNS

1. Stop the burning process with copious amounts of water.

2. Remove burned clothing and restrictive jewelry and such.

3. Gently wash burn with warm water and mild soap, and pat dry.

4. Avoid breaking blisters open, but if they break, remove the skin.

5. Cover burns with ointment and a dry, clean dressing.

6. Watch for respiratory distress.

7. Watch for shock.

8. Evacuate if needed.

Chapter 7
Injuries to the Head & Face

Ice was forming on the rocky slope called Central Gully at the head of Huntington Ravine. It happens that way some Octobers on Mount Washington. A 20-year-old dayhiker moved off the trail seeking surer footing. She didn't find it. Slipping on a more technical section of the ravine, she tumbled about 100 feet, and finished in a free fall of 40 feet. Somewhere on the way down her face struck forcefully against stone. Her boyfriend ran for help.

The first responder arrived from the Appalachian Mountain Club approximately one hour later. He found her barely conscious, her eyes swollen shut, and cerebrospinal fluid (CSF) leaking from her nose. The responder radioed for immediate assistance and, realizing the possibilities, asked for a helicopter. We came on foot another hour further into the incident, and assessed her as critical.

With the patient packaged securely in a rigid basket litter, we began the first of a series of six Z-drags that brought her eventually to the top of the ravine. It was more complicated to haul her up than down, but the nearest landing spot for the 'copter was a flat upper meadow.

Long after dark, she was lifted off for a quick flight to Boston. Extensive surgery was required, but she was able to return finally to a full and healthy life. The serious and often subtle complications of a severe head injury usually cause death in as little as four hours. Separating life and death for this young woman was early recognition of the seriousness of her accident.

Head Injury

The bulk of your brain is the cerebrum, the gray matter, the center of higher functions like thought and emotion. In the back of your head, beneath the cerebrum, is the cerebellum, where equilibrium and coordination are controlled. The brain stem grows out of the base of the brain and is responsible for vital vegetative functions, including circulation and respiration. Enclosing the brain and the spinal cord are three blood-rich layers of tissue called collectively the meninges. Their names, from the brain outward, are the pia mater, arachnoid and dura mater. Cerebrospinal fluid, constantly filling the spaces between the meninges and bathing the brain and spinal cord, is a clear liquid protecting and feeding the central nervous system.

Your brain sits about one millimeter from the inside of your skull, comfortably in command of everything that goes on within you if the temperature, water, blood sugar and pressure stay balanced in your head. Head trauma ranges from simple scalp damage to severe brain damage. The severity is usually a result of the uncompromising structure of the skull (the cranium)—if the brain starts to swell, it is squashed because there's no room up there for the swelling to take place.

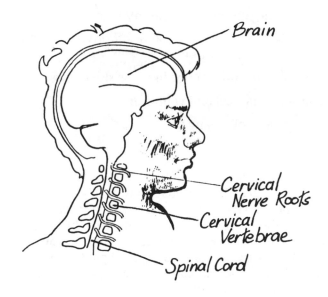

Figure 7-1
Interior arrangement of
the brain and cervical spinal cord.

Assessing Head Injury

For quick reference, head injuries can be loosely divided into three categories:

1) NO LOSS OF CONSCIOUSNESS means only an extremely rare chance of serious problems, despite the fact heavy bleeding and a huge goose-egg sized bump may accompany the injury. Treat open wounds appropriately (see *Wound Management*). You can ice-pack lumps on the head. Keep an eye on the patient for about 24 hours, and evacuate if the signs and symptoms of brain damage develop (see below).

2) SHORT-TERM LOSS OF CONSCIOUSNESS tells that the victim's brain underwent some transient loss of function. This is called a concussion, although a concussion does not always produce loss of consciousness. Keep in mind victims may not be aware they have been unconscious. Ask witnesses, if possible. People knocked unconscious a few minutes are often okay, but they may only appear okay initially, and then start to deteriorate. Watch for 24 hours, awakening the patient several times during the first night.

Evacuate if signs and symptoms of brain damage develop:

1. Distinct changes in personality or sustained disorientation.

2. A headache that increases in intensity.

3. Complaints of blurred vision or other visual disturbances extending over one hour.

4. Excessive or unusual tiredness or sleepiness.

5. Protracted nausea and vomiting.

6. Unusual loss of balance.

7. Seizures.

3) LONG-TERM LOSS OF CONSCIOUSNESS is a serious warning that the brain may be damaged. The problem may be a bruise to the brain, or a tear in the blood vessels of the meninges, or a laceration of the brain itself. The tough dura mater may be clinging to the inside of the cranium, with blood collecting between the dura and the bone (an epidural hematoma). A subdural hematoma is blood pooling between the dura and the brain. The blood can gather over hours, or weeks, increasing the pressure until death results.

Obvious evidence of serious head trauma with a need for rapid evacuation includes:

1. Distinct changes in mental status, often from disoriented to irritable to combative to coma.

2. Depressed fracture of the skull.

3. Visible fracture lines where a portion of the scalp has been torn away.

4. Black-and-blue around swollen eyes (raccoon eyes).

5. Black-and-blue behind and below the ears (Battle's sign).

6. Blood and/or cerebrospinal fluid leaking from the nose or ears.

7. Seizures.

8. Pupils that become distinctly unequal.

9. A heart rate that slows and bounds.

10. Noticeably irregular breathing, often progressing to deep and sighing respirations.

11. Unusual rigid postures.

Treating Head Injuries

To be safe, monitor closely for 24 hours anyone who has received a severe blow to the head. Evacuate to professional medical attention anyone who has been forcefully knocked unconscious if any signs and symptoms of brain damage develop.

MAXIM:
EVACUATE IMMEDIATELY ANYONE KNOCKED
UNCONSCIOUS WHO SHOWS EVIDENCE OF BRAIN DAMAGE

The patient can walk out if capable, and if the spine is cleared (see *Spinal Cord Injury Management*). Remember: Any blow to the head that produces unconsciousness could have damaged the cervical spine. If spine damage is suspected, and/or if brain damage is obvious (see above), keep patients prone. If patients must be left alone for any reason, roll them carefully into a stable side position (the recovery position) to ensure an airway. Deeply unconscious people lose muscle tone, including the tongue which can fall back over the airway. Head-injured people like to vomit, sometimes on a regular basis, and aspirated vomitus (vomit sucked into the lungs) usually causes death. Keep the patient prone on a slope if you can with the head slightly uphill. You may be able to reduce the swelling rate of the brain with gravity's aid.

Figure 7-2
Recovery position to maintain an open airway.

Artificial respiration may be necessary to keep the patient adequately oxygenated. Breathe for any head-injury patient who has a substantially altered level of consciousness and who is breathing outside of normal limits.

Once in a hospital, even seriously head-injured patients have a great chance of survival. Oxygen therapy, drug therapy and surgical intervention are available. That's why they keep the patients awake or arouse them regularly. If arousal is impossible, it is time for radical procedures. In a backcountry situation, let your patient sleep if he or she wants to. In sleep, the brain will have the best chance of controlling its own swelling. Continue monitoring the patient during sleep.

Deep in the wilderness, serious head injuries are a serious threat to life. Given the time and distance from help, you may be called upon to make a tough decision. Should you carry victims out the best you can? Should you go for assistance? There are no absolute answers! If your patients are showing signs of improvement after 48 hours, their prognosis is very good.

The Barehanded Principles:

HEAD INJURY

1. Maintain an airway. Beware of vomiting.
2. Keep head-injury victims on their side if necessary.
3. Evacuate all suspects of brain damage.
4. Let victims sleep if they want to.
5. Treat for possible cervical spine injury, if indicated.

Injuries to the Face

The greatest danger from an injury to the face, whether it be soft tissue damage or fractures of the facial bones, is obstruction of the patient's airway. Management of any face injury needs to include a careful watch to keep the airway clear and the assumption that the cervical spine is damaged until evidence indicates otherwise. This might mean carefully arranging your patients on their side if they're unconscious to let blood flow out of the airway instead of down their windpipe.

The Ear

That flap of flesh, the external ear directs sound down a canal to the eardrum, the tympanic membrane, where the vibrations are transmitted to the three little bones of the middle ear. A tube leads from the middle ear to the nose, balancing the pressure and allowing you the interesting pastime of pinching your nose and blowing to make your ears pop as the pressure changes. The little bones pass the vibrations on to the snail-shaped cochlea of the inner ear which breaks the sound up before sending it along nerve pathways to the brain for decoding.

An injury to the ear will probably be obvious external damage that is treated as any soft tissue injury is handled, or a ruptured eardrum, or a foreign object stuck up the ear canal. Damage to the eardrum can be caused by a blow to the side of the head, a change in pressure while diving underwater, a nearby explosion (possible in a lightning strike). The patient will complain of pain, ringing or whistling in the ear, or loss of hearing, and maybe a loss of coordination (an upsetting phenomenon called vertigo). Keep the ear covered to reduce the chance of infection. Evacuation will depend on the level of pain and discomfort the patient is experiencing.

With the exception of insects, any foreign object lodged in the ear should be removed by a physician. Insects can be drowned with water, alcohol or vegetable or mineral oils. Once dead, the insect will ooze out with the oil or drop out later.

If there's a possibility of a related head injury, do not try to stop the flow of blood from the inside of an injured ear. Patients may be relieving their own increasing intracranial pressure. Cover the ear with bulky sterile dressings to prevent further contamination without stopping the flow.

The Eye

The eyeball is truly round, but only a small slice shows to the outside world. A jelly-like fluid called vitreous humor fills the ball. A bulge, the cornea, sits on the front of the eyeball and is filled with salty fluid called aqueous humor. Between the bulge and the ball lies the lens. Over the lens is a special muscle, the iris, that has an adjustable opening, the pupil. Working together, they focus images on a layer of sensitive cells, the retina, covering the back of the eye. Translated into electrical signals and carried by the optic nerves from each eye to the back of the brain, the image is decoded into thought. Since the images are translated from the back of the brain, sometimes a blow to the back of the head causes visual disturbances.

Nature has determined to protect our eyes in several ways. The outside of the ball, except over the cornea, is covered with a tough membrane called the sclera, the "white" of the eye. A thin, mucous membrane, the conjunctiva, covers the exposed part of the eye and the inner side of the eyelid. Together these see-through "skins" are much hardier than the skin that covers the rest of our bodies. Lacrimal (tear) glands keep the eye moist, washing out most of the dust and debris. The eyelids add protection and help keep the surface of the eye clean when you blink. A bony socket, the orbit, surrounds everything and forms a protective shield. It is lined with fatty "shock absorbers," a final barrier against physical abuse. Still, it is possible to injure the eye.

Foreign Matter in the Eye

The most common problem is when something is in your eye that doesn't belong: debris, hair, insects. The discomfort can be enormous, but usually the victim's own tearing mechanism will wash the eye clean before any serious damage occurs. Healthy first aid is simply to avoid rubbing the eye and immediately washing it out with a lot of clean water. Have the patient lie down while you pour steady stream of water on the bridge of the nose. Rapid blinking encourages the flushing process.

There is nothing harmful about removing large chunks of debris from an eye, as long as force is never used. If the matter does not come loose with the aid of a soft tissue or additional rinsing, leave it alone, cover the eye with a folded gauze pad or sterile eye patch, and get to a doctor. Also, never try to remove anything stuck to the surface of the cornea.

Occasionally the eye will feel irritated after the matter has been removed, making it painful to blink. Most likely, the eye has suffered an abrasion. Rinse the eye again, and if still uncomfortable, patch it shut.

Take an anti-inflammatory analgesic like ibuprofen. Ophthalmic ointment or drops will often provide relief. For irritation that is unrelieved in 24 hours, head for a doctor.

Contusions

The classic "black eye" is a result of rapid swelling and discoloration following a blow. The whites may also turn an alarming red. But don't worry. A cold compress will reduce the pain and swelling. Within 12 to 24 hours the eye will look relatively normal in size. It can take a week to 10 days for the "black" to fade.

Reasons to see a doctor after a punch in the eye include persistent blurred vision, double vision, extraordinary sensitivity to light, and discharge of something other than tears.

Punctures

An eyeball impaled with a sharp object is a serious injury. If the object is still there, do not try to remove it. Keep the patient lying down to prevent gravity from pulling the critically important vitreous humor out.

Stabilizing what has pierced the eye is necessary. One way to do this is to make a "doughnut" out of a rolled handkerchief or triangular bandage. Place it gently around the eye, adding a cup over the doughnut so nothing can catch or jar the object. Tape it all securely, and patch the other eye shut as well. If the good eye looks around nervously, the bad eye will try to follow it, possibly causing more damage. Carry the patient to a hospital if possible.

Laceration of the Eyelid

A cut in the lid produces a lot of blood. Relax, and check the eyeball for damage. If it has been cut, the patient must be kept still and lying down, with both eyes patched. Otherwise, cover the wound with a light, sterile dressing. Although the slice may be quite small, a scar on the eyelid can be a discomfort for the rest of your life. Doctors can stitch the wound neatly with little or no noticeable scarring.

The Nose

Nose injuries usually produce one or two similar manifestations: pain and blood. Keep the patient sitting up and leaning slightly forward, if possible, to prevent blood from entering the airway. If blood is visibly running out, pinch the nostrils closed, using direct pressure to promote clotting. Try to prevent your patient from moving around for about a half hour after the bleeding stops to give clotting a chance to complete. Instruct your patient to please restrain from nose picking, sneezing, and bending over and straining for the next couple of days.

A nose bleed (epistaxis) is almost always anterior. A few, especially in people with chronic high blood pressure, may be posterior. The blood runs down the throat, and the patient may require a doctor's care to stop the bleeding. Decongestant nasal sprays may help reduce bleeding.

Susceptible people have more nose bleeds in dry weather. Applications of an ointment inside the nose can reduce the dryness and prevent bleeds. The same stuff you use on dry lips will work if gently applied to the inside of the nose once or twice a day.

To avoid the possibility of serious damage, an object securely wedged inside a nose should be left in place until a physician can remove it.

Rapid swelling often makes it difficult to make an assessment of a broken nose. If you aren't sure, give the patient painkillers and apply cold packs for 20 to 30 minutes, three or four times a day. If the patient's level of discomfort is acceptable, it's okay to stay in the backcountry. When the nose is obviously broken, the same treatment is advisable, but consider evacuation to a medical facility as well. Your patient may wish to have a bit of surgery done so the nose eventually looks the same as before. There is no rush. The surgery will be just as successful if a week goes by first. In fact, some surgeons like to have the patient wait until the swelling goes down, since it's easier to tell where to realign the nose.

The Mouth

A profusion of blood vessels in the mouth leads to an abundance of bleeding from even very trivial wounds to that area. Active bleeding from mouth trauma almost always stops on its own, and immediate care of the patient should center on maintaining an open airway.

Mouth lacerations tend to look horrible for the first couple of days, but they also tend to heal nicely with little care. The patient should rinse his or her mouth with water every two or three hours and after every meal until the wound is completely closed.

If the wound gapes open significantly, the patient should be evacuated from the backcountry for stitches, especially if the lips are involved. Gaping wounds to the mouth and lips that heal puckered are unsightly, in the way, and difficult to repair once they heal that way (see *Dental Emergencies* for the treatment of injuries involving the teeth).

Chapter 8
Chest Injuries

Leaving the groomed slope for the trees was not her idea. She intended to curve gracefully down to the lodge on one final run. But a combination of fatigue and ice sent her off route and into a high speed collision with a sturdy white pine.

Labored breathing claimed the immediate attention of her rescuers. It was difficult for her to find a position of comfort, and she squirmed in the snow, moaning vigorously. A quick secondary assessment showed an angulated upper left arm and remarkable pain in her pelvis. Her vital signs indicated she was considering going into the progressive stage of shock.

The sled held a full spine board, and even though it was well padded, she complained of the pain of being stabilized on it. Her breathing decreased in quality and increased in rate. Her anxiety increased.

At the hut, supplemental oxygen was started at a high flow, but her level of consciousness continued to decrease on the long ski out. Her short, gasping respirations could be heard above the sound of skis cutting the hard snow. At the ambulance she responded only to painful stimulus.

The hospital's x-rays revealed neat fractures of the arm and pelvis, easily treated. Of more critical concern were the splinters of bone from three shattered ribs on the left side. At least one piece of bone had punctured a lung. Air leaking out of the lung was filling her chest cavity and making it more and more difficult to adequately exchange oxygen. Her full recovery would have been impossible without rapid surgical intervention.

How We Breathe

Our breathing apparatus is composed partly of twelve pairs of ribs. All are firmly attached in back to vertebrae, and the top ten adhere to the sternum in front. The last two float freely low in the chest. A dome-shaped muscle, the diaphragm, is curved along the lower line of the ribs, separating the lungs and heart from the lower organs. The lungs are five spongy lobes, three on our right and two on our left, made up of thousands of tiny grape-like clusters of alveoli bunched at the end of bronchioles. A tough membrane, the visceral pleura, surrounds each lung. A continuation of the membrane, the parietal pleura, lines the inner chest wall. Between the two membranes is a *potential* space, the pleural cavity, which should remain potential because the lungs are designed to stick to the inside of the rib cage.

On inspiration the muscles between the ribs flex and the ribs are pulled upward. The diaphragm flexes and thus flattens, pulling downward. The lungs slide along the inner chest wall, but are forced open since a fluid keeps them from pulling away. A "vacuum" is created inside the chest, and air rushes in through the nose or mouth, down the windpipe to where it divides into a right and left bronchus, into bronchioles of ever-decreasing size until it reaches a sac of alveoli. At the alveoli, oxygen in the air is exchanged for carbon dioxide in the blood, and life goes on. Inspiration is the active phase of breathing.

On expiration the muscles relax, returning to their normal position. The elastic tissues of the lungs are pulled back to their original position. Air is pushed out. Expiration is the passive phase of breathing.

Figure 8-1
Interior arrangement of the chest.

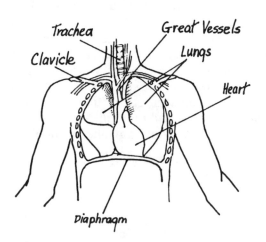

Chest Injuries

An injury to the chest can be closed, the damage done inside the patient without anything penetrating the integrity of the chest wall. The injury can be open, the result of the forceful entry of an object.

Fractured Ribs

Breaking a rib or two is the most common injury to the chest, and the fifth to the tenth ribs are most commonly involved. The first four are protected by the shoulder, and the freedom in front enjoyed by the last two allow them to absorb more of a blow.

Patients complain of localized pain after receiving a direct hit on the chest wall. They like to sit hunched forward, their arms protectively holding the injury, breathing shallowly to ease the discomfort.

The pain may be great, but if the fracture is simple and uncomplicated the patient may safely choose to stay in the backcountry. Whether they stay or go, a sling and swathe on the injured side often eases the discomfort by supporting the muscles that spasm and cause the pain. Any activity aggravating the injury should be avoided, and it is best to see a physician once one is available. Monitor closely for signs of underlying damage.

Pneumothorax

Air (pneumo) enters the chest (thorax), which sounds like a healthy occurrence, except this air is entering the pleural space from a tear in the lung made by a complicated fractured rib. The vacuum between the visceral and parietal pleura is destroyed, and, as air collects in the no-longer-potential space, the lung eventually collapses. Patients have more and more difficulty breathing. Their hearts tend to speed up as their level of anxiety rises. Suspect this injury in anyone who has received a blow to the chest and demonstrates increasing respiratory distress.

These patients needs a physician as soon as possible. It will be best if they are carried. Walking will increase their need for oxygen and complicate their breathing. They will usually travel easiest in a semi-sitting position.

Tension Pneumothorax

Excessive air pressure in the pleural cavity makes it impossible for the patient to adequately breathe. The heart, trachea (windpipe), and large blood vessels of the chest are pushed toward the uninjured side by the increasing pressure. The injured side of the chest becomes rigid and distended. Watch for the signs and symptoms of shock.

Death results unless a qualified person opens an appropriate hole in the injured chest to relieve the pressure. It is best to try to anticipate the development of a tension pneumothorax, and start an evacuation as soon as possible.

Spontaneous Pneumothorax

Someone with emphysema or another lung disease, or a person who is otherwise predisposed (e.g. an active young person that grew tall rapidly), may develop a pneumothorax spontaneously, without trauma to the chest. A lung suddenly ruptures, allowing air into the pleural space. Sudden stabbing chest pain and increasing difficulty breathing should create suspicion of this condition.

Hemothorax

Damage to the chest may result in an accumulation of blood in the chest cavity. A hemothorax often occurs simultaneously with a pneumothorax. The blood collects in the lower area of the lung, and may be difficult if not impossible to assess. Management of the patient will be the same as for pneumothorax.

Contusions

A blow to the chest may bruise the heart or lungs. The result may be chest pain and the signs and symptoms of shock with disturbances in the rhythm of the heart (bruised heart) or respiratory distress with a cough that produces blood (lung bruise). General principles for treating a chest injury should be followed. If patients feel like coughing up blood, encourage them to do so. This helps keep their lungs free of excess fluid.

Pericardial Tamponade

Around the heart lies a tough membrane called the pericardial sac (or pericardium). Trauma to the chest may cause a tear in the heart, allowing blood to leak out and fill the sac. The heart is compressed and each succeeding beat is less efficient than the one before. The heart beats faster and more weakly as the pressure on it increases. The patient grows increasingly anxious and short of breath. It is not easy to assess pericardial tamponade. If the blood pressure can be checked, a drop in systolic will be noted with a corresponding slight rise in diastolic. As with any serious chest injury, the patient needs surgical intervention to live.

Flail

A flail is a free-floating piece of chest wall created when three or more adjacent ribs are broken in two or more places. The result is paradoxical respiration, the free piece moving in opposition to the rest of the chest. Pain is great, and difficulty breathing is extreme. As with any suspicion of serious chest injury, take a look at the patient's chest. Here you will see deformity and, eventually, the paradoxical movement—maybe not at first when muscle spasms hold the flail in place, but certainly later as the muscles fatigue. Asking the patient to inhale deeply will allow you to assess pain and deformity early.

A flail creates a dire emergency. Oxygen demands cannot be met by the inadequate respiration, and respiratory failure is not far away. Underlying damage is common.

Immediate management is the only hope of saving these patients. If they are unconscious, roll them on to their injured side, hoping to reduce some of the movement of the flail. This "recovery position" helps keep their airway open as well. If the respiratory distress becomes acute, start rescue breathing. If they stop living, do CPR. Evacuation to a medical facility is, of course, essential.

Sucking Chest Wound
The sucking noise is made by air being pulled into the pleural space by the pressure of inhalation because something from the outside has penetrated the chest wall. This can happen after being shot or stabbed. Sometimes called an open pneumothorax, the air sucked in through the wound is useless, but it takes up the space needed for normal breathing to happen. Air flows in and out of the hole instead of in and out of the normal air passages. The patient rapidly asphyxiates.

Immediately seal the wound with your gloved hand. As soon as possible, make a more permanent cover for the hole with a material that lets no air or water through, like a plastic bag. Tape it down securely on three sides, leaving the fourth side open in hopes the patient will self-relieve a developing pnuemothorax. Keep patients in the position of comfort they choose (which is usually a semi-sitting position). During evacuation, monitor them closely for increasing respiratory distress, a sign they are developing a tension pneumothorax, possible now since you closed their chest. If it happens, tear off the dressing and let the air out of the chest. Clotting may make this difficult without pulling away the clotted blood, or even gently inserting your finger into the hole. With the pressure relieved, replace the seal. Positive pressure ventilation may be necessary.

Impaled Object
If the object puncturing a chest is still there, every attempt should be made to leave it there. Great care should be taken to immobilize it in place since even slight movement may result in further internal damage. Lots of bulky padding will be helpful, as will extreme carefulness in evacuation.

Truthfully, it is not always possible to give a victim ideal treatment. Some people will insist on impaling themselves on the most awkward objects (like stout limbs of trees). Keeping the principles of chest injury management in mind, you may be called upon to do your creative best (e.g. remove the object or cut it down to a manageable size).

The Barehanded Principles:
CHEST INJURY

1. Maintain an open airway.

2. Take a look at the chest.

3. Let conscious patients assume the position of most comfort.

4. Treat the injury you find: Sling and swathe the arm on the side of a fractured rib, positive pressure ventilate the flail, plug sucking chest wounds, immobilize the impaled object.

5. Assist with breathing, if necessary. Any chest-injured patient breathing more than 30 per minute needs rescue breathing at a slower, deeper rate.

6. Carry out all but the most trivial chest injuries.

7. Encourage an occasional deep breath and the coughing up of any accumulating fluids.

Chapter 9
Abdominal Injury & Illness

The call from the lodge said a skier was complaining of severe abdominal pain. He was curled into a comfortable-looking chair, but he was looking uncomfortable. A peek at the area where he said the pain was greatest revealed a bruise over his upper left abdomen, just below the ribs. His breaths came rapid and shallow, his heart raced. He was pale and pasty.

To the question, "What happened?" he described gaining too much air on a jump, losing control, and landing forcefully on his left side. The wind whooshed out of him. He was lean and fit, and, pulling himself together, skied on down for a cup of coffee and the slow onset of shock.

Within two hours of arriving at the local hospital, his ruptured spleen lay in a basin on an operating room table. Without the operation, the same two hours would have been the rest of his life.

Abdominal injuries are typically easier to assess than serious abdominal illnesses (which are often referred to as an acute abdomen), but any abdominal problem tends to involve a search for mysterious clues that leave even a physician baffled. Packed into the region between our diaphragm and our groin are many important parts that can be:

1. Crushed or torn by the force of blunt trauma, creating a closed injury.
2. Penetrated by an object, creating an open injury.
3. Perforated by ulcers, etc.
4. Infected by a variety of organisms.
5. Obstructed by kidney stones, gallstones, fecal impactions, etc.

Some of the parts are solid (pancreas, liver, kidneys, spleen) and mostly tucked under the rib cage for more protection, and some are hollow (stomach, intestines, gallbladder, urinary bladder, female reproductive organs). The lining of the abdominal cavity is a membrane called the peritoneum. Officially, the cavity has three parts: the abdomen, the retroperitoneum (the space behind the peritoneum where the kidneys and pancreas sit), and the subperitoneum (or pelvic region). Your treatment will not be hindered if you simply think of it as "the abdomen." But it will help in your assessment to know generally where the organs are supposed to be.

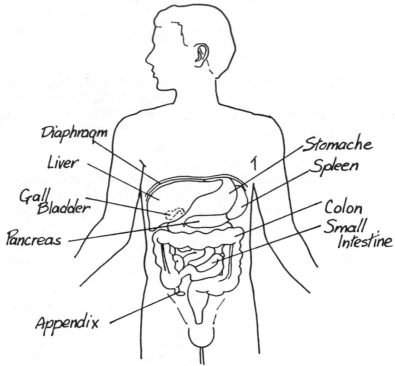

Figure 9-1
Interior arrangement of the abdomen.

Abdominal Assessment

1. Look at the abdomen with the patient lying down. A normal abdomen is gently rounded and symmetrical. Look for distention, bruises and obvious injuries.

2. Ask the patient about his or her condition. Has this ever happened before? Does anything provoke the pain? make it better? make it worse?

What is its quality? (Ask the patient to describe the discomfort.) Has it begun to radiate from the original pain site? Evaluate the severity (on a scale of one to ten). What time did the pain start? Did it start suddenly? These are the PQRST questions of patient assessment.

3. Feel (palpate) the abdomen with flat fingers. Press gently in all four quadrants of the abdomen. Watch for a pain response. Normal abdomens are soft and not tender. Feel for rigid muscles, lumps and pain specific to a local spot.

4. Listen with an ear (or stethoscope) pressed against each of the four quadrants. This takes time. In two or three minutes, within each quadrant, bowel sounds (gurgling noises) should be heard. Absence of noise means something is not working right.

Blunt Trauma

The victim of a severe blow to the abdomen needs to have an adequate history taken since what has taken place inside is not very obvious. What hit him? How fast was it going? Where is the pain?

When you press gently on the abdomen during your examination, the patient may reflexively "guard"—a sign of a serious abdominal problem. When you palpate the abdomen, you may feel unusual lumps. When you look at the abdomen, you may see bruising.

Solid organs bleed when ruptured. Since blood is less irritating than hollow-organ contents the signs and symptoms of peritonitis (see below) may not appear. The signs and symptoms of shock may appear. You should also see increasing rigidity, distention, and pain in the abdomen, and possibly the loss of bowel sounds. Threat to life may be immediate.

Trauma that tears open internal organs releases whatever the organ held. For hollow organs it may be things like stomach acid, digested food or bacteria. Hollow-organ contents are highly irritating. They cause an inflammatory reaction in the peritoneum called peritonitis. Pain may be described as sharp, stabbing or burning, and it increases and spreads throughout the abdomen. Pulse and respiration quicken. The muscles of the abdomen become increasingly rigid and distended. Your ear placed against the patient's abdomen, periodically, reveals a decrease in the gurgles and rumbles of normal bowel activity as the intestines become paralyzed. The patient will lie very still on his back or side but demand flexion of his knees to take pressure off his abdominal muscles. Pain is provoked by movement and any attempt to straighten the legs.

With any abdominal injury anticipate nausea and vomiting. Over time, blood may appear in the vomit, urine or stool of the patient. He may develop a fever.

Penetrating Injuries

In the backcountry, the penetrating object could be a knife or gun, an ice axe or a ski pole, etc. The immediate seriousness of the injury, as with blunt trauma, is determined by what got damaged inside and how bad it's bleeding. With severe bleeding, shock is imminent, and immediate evacuation the only chance of salvation. Over time the risk of infection is very high. General assessment of the patient is the same as with a closed injury. Treatment will vary somewhat depending on the soft tissue involvement. Impaled objects should be stabilized in place (see *Wound Management*). Rapid, but extremely gentle, evacuation is warranted.

An evisceration is a specific type of injury that opens the abdomen and lets intestines protrude. In short-term care, cover the exposed bowels with sterile dressings soaked in disinfected water to prevent drying out. Check the dressings every two hours to make sure they stay moist. Cover the moist dressings with thick, dry dressings, and rapidly evacuate the patient. In long-term care, over several hours, the exposed intestines will do better if they are flushed clean with disinfected water and "teased" back inside by gently pulling the wound open. Dress the wound and evacuate the patient expediently.

Perforations

Patients with ulcers usually can describe a history of stomach problems. Pain may be a burning, stinging fire or a gnawing ache, and may be in the upper abdomen or migrating to the back. When the patient eats or takes an antacid, the pain of a ulcer usually subsides—just the opposite for indigestion, which usually comes on when the patient eats. If the pain doesn't go away with food and antacids, it's time for an evacuation. The patient can usually walk.

Infections

Serious abdominal infections will produce a persistent high fever—102° F or more—along with the pain. Any movement increases the pain. Illnesses such as appendicitis often create a "stomachache" that becomes increasingly localized over a period of a day or two in the infected organ (in the lower right quadrant of the abdomen). Nausea and vomiting are expected. When you press on the abdomen over an infected organ, the patient may complain of pain when you release the pressure, a phenomenon called "rebound tenderness." Abdominal infections need a physician's attention as soon as possible.

Obstructions

Abdominal obstructions usually produce localized pain. Kidney stones usually produce excruciating pain beneath the lower ribs in back, where the kidneys are located, and moves down the ureters with increasing intensity as the stone moves down. The patient often complains of pain radiating into the lower abdomen. Blood may appear in the urine. Kidney stones are often passed after a day of agonizing misery. Fecal impactions are often assessed by asking when the last bowel movement occurred, and by palpating a lump in the lower left quadrant. Waves of severe cramping may occur. Severe fecal impactions have to be manually removed. All "obstructed" patients should be kept well-hydrated. Relief may come with medications for pain. Persistent pain, over 24 hours, should be investigated by a physician.

Signs & Symptoms of Serious Abdominal Pain

With so many problems to choose from, you may find it impossible to assess the exact cause of the pain. There are, however, indications that the patient's condition, no matter the cause, warrants a rapid evacuation.

1. Signs and symptoms of progressive shock.

2. Fever at or above 102° F.

3. More than 24 hours of persistent pain.

4. More than 24 hours of persistent nausea, vomiting or diarrhea.

5. Localized pain, as opposed to general "stomachache."

6. Description of pain: burning, stinging, fiery pain that increases in intensity.

7. Blood: from the mouth, in vomit (often appearing like coffee grounds), in the urine (pale pinkish), from the rectum, or in the stool (often appearing like tar).

8. Persistent unwillingness to move, along with "guarding" the abdomen.

General Treatment

Patients with abdominal pain should be kept in the position of comfort they choose, and kept warm. If you are involved in their evacuation, comfort and warmth should be extended to them during the carry. Monitor them for the vomit that commonly appears, and be sure it is kept out of their airway. In general, nothing should be given to them by mouth unless the patients' chief complaint is diarrhea and/or vomiting, in which case hydration is indicated. (Note: On an extended evacuation, with any serious abdominal problem, sips of cold water may be necessary to prevent dehydration.) Mild abdominal discomfort can be treated with some medications (see *Common Simple Problems*).

Serious abdominal injuries and illnesses need rapid evacuation. The evacuation should be as gentle as possible. Often surgical intervention is all that will eventually prevent untimely death.

The Barehanded Principles:
ABDOMINAL INJURY & ILLNESS

1. Assess for seriousness of injury or illness.

2. Keep the patient in the chosen position of comfort, and keep warm.

3. Watch for vomiting, protect from aspiration if vomiting occurs, and maintain the airway.

4. Control obvious bleeding, and manage open wounds appropriately.

5. Evacuate the seriously ill or injured patient as soon as possible, in a position of comfort, being careful to avoid undue movement.

6. Watch for shock.

Chapter 10
Athletic Injuries

David chose to ride his mountain bike along the old cross-country trail. It was too good a day to stay inside. Spring green blurred the distance in a vernal mist. The snow was gone, and the leaves were slick and matted to the ground after their recent burial. There was a pitch where the creek jumped off a rock face, necessitating portage, but otherwise the ride was long and relatively flat, and just right for getting out quick. David was alone again, as he often preferred.

Tired and a bit out of shape, he pushed too hard on the return run to asphalt. A half-mile out, where the trail cornered, he lost traction in a patch of wet leaves. Throwing his right leg out for support, his ankle rolled and exploded in pain. He tried to stop the ground from coming up so fast, but something popped in his right wrist. For a few minutes he lay on the soggy carpet, wishing his ankle belonged to someone else.

The most immediate question was: How serious is it? Probing around the ankle with his healthy hand, David found nothing saying broken bone, no unusual movement, no numbness or tingling in his foot, no exceptional feeling of cold, nothing to distinguish one ankle from the other . . . except the pain. Strain, sprain, or fracture, all serious musculoskeletal injuries have one thing in common—they are too painful to use. Intuitively, David trusted his ankle. He tried it, and it still worked. And so did his wrist. He rode out slowly, packed the bike on top of his car, and drove the ten miles home for a hot shower and dinner.

Next morning, the swelling and discoloration in his ankle would've made his own mother turn away. His wrist was sore but functional. Mismanagement had turned a minor injury into a big problem. A couple of days ago, over two years since the accident, David sat by my fire chatting. He complained of the soreness in his right ankle.

Strains

A strain is a stretch in a muscle and/or the tendons that attach muscles to bones. Strains can be debilitating, especially in the lower back. In general, strains can be treated the same as sprains (see below). Should you treat them with heat or cold? Cold should be applied for 20 to 30 minutes, several times a day, for the first 48 hours. After two days, heat works best for strains in most cases. A couple of days of rest are the preferred treatment for back pain—rest on your side, or on your back with high padding beneath your knees. Massages often help. The muscle can be used within the limits of pain. In other words: If it hurts, don't do it!

Reasons to evacuate your patient for medical attention include: 1) the pain (or numbness), especially in the back, begins to radiate all the way down an arm or leg; 2) the pain remains strong even when the muscles are at rest; 3) the pain starts as a result of illness; and 4) the pain comes on sharply after a fall from a height or a sudden jolting stop.

Sprains

Sprains are injuries to ligaments, the bands holding joints together, and can vary in degree from simple over-stretching to complete tears. Unlike fractures that mend strong, and strains that heal well, a sprain is likely to bother you for the rest of your life, especially if you treat it improperly. What's really unfortunate about these injuries is that they don't hurt as much as they should. Pain would encourage us to act sensibly. Sensible action has three stages: first aid, rest and retraining.

Our first response is critical. Every minute RICE is delayed can add an hour to healing. RICE is an acronym for Rest, Ice, Compression and Elevation. Stay off the injury (*Rest*) for the first half hour while you reduce its temperature. *Ice* as much as possible without freezing. Crushed ice is best. It conforms to the shape of the anatomy involved. Do not put the ice directly on skin since that could produce a cold injury. Wrap the ice with a shirt or sock. Without ice, soak in cold water, or carry chemical cold packs in your first-aid kit, or (during warm months) submerge the joint in a wet T-shirt or something else made of cotton, and let evaporation cool the damaged area. *Compression* requires an elastic bandage (e.g. Ace). Wrap it snug, but watch it carefully for loss of circulation—tingling, numbness, and pain due to over-aggressive compression. *Elevation* refers to keeping the injury higher than the patient's heart. After RICE-ing, let rewarming happen naturally for 10-15 minutes before trying to use the joint, to prevent further damage the ice-induced anesthesia might allow. Monitor the amount of swelling and discoloration.

MAXIM:

THE DEGREE OF SWELLING AND DISCOLORATION
INDICATES THE DEGREE OF DAMAGE

The goal of RICE is to limit swelling. The more the injury swells, the less you move it. The less you move, the quicker the muscles deteriorate. The faster the muscle atrophies, the longer it takes to heal. Over the next 48 hours, you do want use the injury as little as possible, keep the compression on, repeat the icing regularly (three or four times per day).

But as soon as the swelling stops getting worse, start exercising the joint. Wiggle it gently—for example, spell the alphabet in the air with toes. Add mild heat to loosen the stiffness, but warm up the water no hotter than a few degrees above body temperature. If swelling starts to increase, go back to cold. But keep up the exercising as much as pain will allow. You are increasing circulation to carry off the excess fluid and dead cells surrounding the injury, and smoothing out the fibers of the ligaments, and strengthening the muscles. You are speeding healing.

Anti-inflammatory drugs ease the pain as well as reduce the inflammation of athletic injuries. Ibuprofen works best for most people. A recommended dose is 400 milligrams three times per day. Many people do better on higher doses. Consult your physician.

Even a mild sprain will take two months to heal solidly. You may be comfortable in one week and feeling marvelous in two. But do not be fooled. Exercise your injured joint aggressively, but do not push it past the point of pain. If you are worse the next day, retreat, gather your strength, and push forward with more gentleness.

How do you know when you're well? Test your joints independently of each other, increasing the pressure on them slowly. Is your balance the same? Is your strength the same? Does the injured side hurt while the healthy side doesn't? Hop a few times on that sprained ankle. If you can't, you aren't completely healed. When your strength and pain responses are bilaterally equal for approximately ten repetitions of the same movement, you are ready to increase your training schedule.

Shoulders, elbows, wrists, fingers, knees, ankles, toes . . . any joint can be sprained, and the supporting muscles can be strained. The principles for treatment don't change with the body part: a RICE period, a rest period, a retraining period. But stretching and strengthening should be specific to the injured area.

The Ankle

Ankles, by far, are the joint most sprained. After RICE, if the ankle is usable, it would be best to tape it before continuing to use it. Ankle taping is a valuable backcountry medical skill and, as with all skills, you'll get better at it by practicing.

Figure 10-1
Outside or *lateral* view of ankle ligaments.

Tape works and feels best if the ankle is shaved first, or a pre-wrap material (commercially available) is used. But you can tape over a thin liner sock. Plan on using about one roll of one-inch x 10 yards to do one ankle. Tape should be applied snugly, with as few wrinkles as possible. You don't need to tape from toe to calf—mid-foot to a couple of inches above the ankle bones is enough.

Start by marking the boundaries of the ankle taping area with anchors at mid-foot and above the ankle bones. Apply stirrups that pull foot up into the ankle. Then figure-eights that hold the ankle firmly together. Start the "eights" toward the injured side, which is usually the outside of the ankle, to reduce strain on the injured ligaments. After the eights, a heel-lock will add further support. Finish by filling in the empty spaces, but leave the heel free (see Figure 10-2).

Note: Figure-eights can be applied over an elastic wrap or sock if tape is in short supply.

Figure 10-2
Taping the ankle.

The Knee

Knees are the second-most sprained joint. After initial care, they can be splinted in a manner that allows the patient to walk. With a pad behind the knee, Crazy Creek Chairs make great knee splints, wrapped from behind, leaving the kneecap free but taped or tied firmly in place. Sleeping pads work well, too. Roll the pad up from both ends and tape or tie it firmly in place, leaving the kneecap free, with the rolls on each side of the knee (see Figure 10-3).

Figure 10-3
Knee Splint

Figure 10-4
Front or *anterior* view of the knee.

Evacuation

With most injuries, the patient is all the questions and all the answers. With minor musculoskeletal injuries this is very true. Can these patients bear the workload necessary to stay in the backcountry? Can they bear the pressure of the group if they can't keep up? Are they having fun? Do you think they are substantially increasing the risk to themselves or the group? If the patient is mobile, the final decision about whether to evacuate or not will depend on the many parts that make the whole picture.

The Barehanded Principles:

ATHLETIC INJURIES

1. Rest, Ice, Compress and Elevate (RICE) the injury as soon as possible.
2. Let it rewarm naturally for 10 to 15 minutes.
3. Test the injury for seriousness, for usability.
4. If they stay in the backcountry, repeat RICE-ing three to four times per day for at least 48 hours.
5. Tape ankles and splint knees.
6. If the patient is unsafe, unwell or unhappy, evacuate.

Chapter 11
Fractures

Miriam moved down the hard-packed snow slope cautiously. A fierce June sun burned overhead. Her crampons took a solid bite of the glacier, but it was her first time descending steep terrain. Miriam was afraid, wishing she had taken the leader's advice and stayed close to camp. Slipping out on her own, she had found going up easy, and climbed much higher than her original intention.

At least the others could see her. Crowded together near the colorful nylon village of tents, they waved. Their voices of encouragement drifted up muffled and unintelligible. Miriam lifted her ice axe to wave back. It was a mistake. Her tenuous balance gave out under the added stress and she fell to her backside, gaining speed rapidly as she flailed for a brake. By the time she hit the exposed rocks at the end of the glacier, she was moving with enough force to snap her right femur, the large bone of her thigh.

The pain was intense, and swelling started almost immediately. Group members were at her side in moments, and were required to pull traction on her leg. Traction eased the pain, but the slightest movement ripped screams from Miriam. It was impossible to move her more than a few feet.

Before sending for help, a complete assessment was made, checking for any injuries the pain of the broken femur might be masking. A note was written, giving details of who, what, when and where. The note was attached to a marked map, and three well-equipped, strong hikers were sent to request a helicopter. It was fourteen miles to the nearest road.

While the three "runners" were still preparing to leave, the leader rigged an improvised traction splint for Miriam's leg. He sliced the floor of a free-standing tent from end to end and set it up over her. With difficulty, they were able to get her onto a foamlite pad, off the cold surface of the mountain. For two uncomfortable days, the group stayed close to the patient, helping her maintain body warmth, giving her food and water, assisting her as she eliminated her body wastes.

The care Miriam received on the mountain kept her leg intact. Surgical placement of a rod down the inside of her bone was required to complete full healing. But the story could have ended in permanent loss of function, or loss of leg . . . or loss of life.

Assessment

Fractures of bones in the arms and legs make up a large percentage of injuries in the backcountry. Sometimes the assessment is simple: Bones protrude through the skin, or angulations in the bones create joints where there aren't supposed to be any. Without the obvious, and without a radiographic picture of the bones, the rescuer can base the assessment of a fracture on common sense and a good LAF at the injury.

The L of LAF stands for Look. Remove or cut away clothing carefully and take a look at the site of the injury. (In cold weather this cutting away should be kept to a minimum.) Is there discoloration and swelling? Can patients move the injury or do they guard it carefully? Compare the injured side to the uninjured side. Does it look broken?

The A of LAF stands for Ask. Ask patients to rate their pain. Do the patients think they're broken? Did they feel anything break? How did the injury occur? High-speed impacts cause more breaks than low-speed impacts. Torqued bones break more often than straight on impacts. How willing is the patient to use the injury?

The F stands for Feel. Does the area or the areas of the injury feel rigid with spasms of the surrounding muscle? Does it feel unstable? Is there "point tenderness," a place on the bone that hurts noticeably more when you touch that spot? Check for Circulation, Sensation and Motion (CSM) beyond the site of the injury. Loss of pulse, numbness, tingling, and inability to move are signs of loss of adequate blood flow, the most immediately serious complication of a fracture.

MAXIM:

WHEN IN DOUBT, SPLINT

Splinting

The goal of a healthy splint is to immobilize the damaged bone(s), preventing further injury and increasing patient comfort until a medical facility can be reached. To do this best, the splint needs to be made of 1) something well-padded next to the patient and 2)something rigid for additional support. Padding should fill all the spaces within the system to prevent movement of the injury. Avoid the void! In addition, a splint should be long enough to 3) immobilize the joints above and below a fractured bone or immobilize the bones above and below an injured joint.

Splints should immobilize the injured bone in the position of function, or as close to the position of function as possible. Functional position means legs almost straight with a slight flexion at the knee (pad behind the knee), feet at 90 degrees to legs, arms in 90 degrees of flexion, wrists straight, and fingers flexed into a functional curve. A spine, including neck and pelvis, should be splinted straight.

In choosing materials for splinting you are only limited by your imagination. For padding there are sleeping bags, foamlite pads (which you can cut to fit the problem), Crazy Creek Chairs, extra clothing, even soft debris from the forest floor stuffed into clothing if additional padding would be helpful. For rigidity there are sticks, tent poles, ice axes, stays from internal frame packs, ski poles. Some ensolite pads are rigid enough to make a padded splint when folded into place and secured around the arm or leg. Lightweight, commercial splints are available as additions to your backcountry first-aid kit (e.g. SAM splints, wire splints).

Splints can be secured in place with bandanas, strips of clothing, pack straps, belts, and pieces of rope. Useful items from your first-aid kit for securing splints include tape and elastic wraps. Wide elastic wraps (4-6 inches) allow you to provide firm security with little loss of circulation. Large triangular bandages can be very helpful in the creation of slings and swathes.

Specific Fractures: Upper Body

MANDIBLE (jaw): Secure the jaw in place with a wide wrap that goes around the head. Be sure to provide for an adequate airway and a way for patients to quickly remove the wrap should they feel like vomiting (which they often do after a blow to the jaw).

Figure 11-1
Stabilization method for the jaw.

CLAVICLE (collarbone): You can break the thin collarbone with a direct blow or by falling on your arm or shoulder. The pain may be specific to the collarbone or general to the shoulder, and movement makes it worse. The weight of the arm should be held up firmly in a sling. The sling should be secured to the body with swathes to keep the shoulder immobile.

Figure 11-2a
Sling and swathes to stabilize a fractured
clavicle, lower arm, elbow, rib, etc.

HUMERUS (upper arm): The upper arm bone can be broken with a direct blow or a wrenching motion. Pain is usually specific to the damaged area, but the patient may complain of shoulder pain if the fracture is high on the humerus. Let the weight of the lower arm hang in a sling with the elbow free to hang down and pull a little traction of the injured upper arm. Wide wraps around the upper arm and chest secure the fracture to the rigid and well-padded chest wall.

Figure 11-2b
Sling and swathe to stabilize
a fractured humerus.

RADIUS & ULNA (lower arm): A fall or a direct blow to either bone of the lower arm may cause a fracture of one or both. Secure the lower arm to something well-padded and rigid, and secure the splinted arm in a sling with swathes.

Figure 11-3
Splint for the lower arm or wrist.

WRIST: If there is pain and swelling in the wrist, your suspicion of a fracture should be high. The complex structure of the wrist doesn't usually bend too far without breaking. Splint the lower arm, being sure to incorporate the hand. Place a roll or wad of soft material in the hand to keep it flexed into a position of function. Secure the arm in a sling with swathes.

HAND: Same as wrist. Be sure to firmly secure the hand to the splint with a wide wrap.

FINGERS: The injured finger should be taped or wrapped securely to an adjacent finger after placing cotton or gauze between the fingers. Keep the fingers flexed in the normal position of function, not straight.

RIBS: Sling and swathe the arm on the injured side (see *Chest Injuries*).

Specific Fractures: Lower Body

PELVIS: In the backcountry, pelvic fractures are usually the result of falls from a height or high-speed skiing collisions. Pushing gently on the pelvis of the patient produces a marked pain response. Patients don't like to sit up or roll onto their side. There is the possibility of damage to the internal organs and extensive internal bleeding. Pain can sometimes be reduced by wrapping the pelvis snugly. Splinting requires immobilization of the entire spinal column on a well-padded full backboard. Leg and body motion should be kept to a minimum. Sometimes a full backboard can be improvised from boards, straight sticks, or external pack frames lashed firmly together. Going for help is a healthy idea.

HIP: Fractures of the hip are not a common backcountry occurrence. Should it happen, patients complain of pain very high on the femur (thigh) with their leg rolled outward from normal. Compare legs. With gentle traction, pull the leg on the broken side into alignment with the other leg, pad well between the legs, and secure the two legs together. The patient will need to be carried out on a well-padded, rigid litter.

FEMUR (upper leg): This, your largest bone, takes a great deal of force to break. It usually takes a fall from a significant height or a very high-speed collision . . . but not always. There will be considerable pain in the region of the middle of the thigh. There can be considerable bleeding into the thigh. Prompt manual traction on the femur is required to 1) prevent an increase in the severity of the injury (an unstable femur may even be pulled out through the skin by spasms of the muscles), 2) reduce bleeding into the thigh, and 3) reduce the amount of pain the patient is suffering. Unlike other fractures, the traction cannot be released after the tension is relieved in the muscle. The large thigh muscles may re-spasm violently.

Treatment of a fractured femur requires a device to maintain traction on the leg. Commercial products are available (e.g. Kendrick Traction Device or KTD), but with creativity such a device can be improvised in the backcountry. While one rescuer maintains the manual traction, another gathers the material. MAINTAIN TRACTION UNTIL A FEMUR TRACTION SPLINT IS IN PLACE. There are numerous ways to create a traction splint, some on the outside of the leg and some on the inside. Here is a simple method that works:

1. Secure a fixation splint firmly to the injured leg (e.g. foamlite pad). This will provide support of the fracture and patient comfort while the traction device is being improvised and after the device is in place.

2. A strip of something long and soft needs to be tied around the ankle on the injured leg with a loop at the sole of the foot (see below).

3. A shaft about one foot longer than the injured leg needs to be found. This can be a stick, a ski pole, a tent pole, a paddle.

4. One end should be very well padded. Sometimes the patient's shoe can be used for this pad. Secure the pad very well on the end of the shaft, and place the padded end gently in the patient's groin. The patient may need a lot of reassurance. Secure the shaft in place near the groin level with a wrap around the patient's upper thigh.

5. A piece of rope, cord, or strong cloth is needed to make a trucker's hitch. Traction by the trucker's hitch is pulled from the loop at the sole of the foot and the end of the shaft until the traction of the device is equal or greater than the manual traction. The best judge of the amount of traction is the patient, who usually offers this judgment without your asking for it.

6. When mechanical traction is secure, pad between the shaft and the leg, and use enough wraps of cloth or elastic bandages to secure the shaft firmly in place. An elastic wrap around the fracture site will help reduce pain and bleeding. With a small pad in the groin, the bad leg can be secured to the good leg for additional support.

Figure 11-4
Ankle hitch.

Figure 11-5
Trucker's hitch.

If you find yourself alone with a victim suffering a fractured femur, you'll have to forego manual traction, gather the materials, and carefully apply mechanical traction when everything is in place. A rigid litter is usually required to get the patient out of the backcountry. The patient needs a hospital as soon as possible to prevent permanent loss of function or loss of leg.

Figure 11-6
Improvised traction device for fractured femur.

STRAPS ON BOTH SIDES OF FX SITE

TOE OF BOOT OPENED TO ACCESS PULSE

TRACTION (12" MIN. NEEDED)

TRACTION SPLINT SECURED AT THIGH

EXTRA PADDING AT THIGH

INSULITE TYPE PAD ROLLED + SECURED AROUND THE INJURED LEG

PATELLA (kneecap): This is usually the result of a blow to the knee or falling on the knee. With a soft pad under the knee to keep the knee slightly flexed, the leg will need to be splinted. The knee often likes to be wrapped in a circular splint, one that wraps around the whole leg. Sleeping pads can work very well for this type of splint.

TIBIA & FIBULA (lower leg): Lower leg fractures are most often the result of a high impact accident. The majority of backcountry evacuations for a musculoskeletal injury will be for a lower leg injury (knee, tibia, fibula, ankle). The splint should incorporate the knee and the ankle. Soft padding under the knee keeps the patient more comfortable. The rigidity should be concentrated under the leg where gravity's pull will be felt. A sleeping pad wrapped around the leg from above the knee and including the ankle, tied firmly in place, will often suffice. AVOID THE VOIDS.

Figure 11-7
Improvised lower leg splint from an ensolite pad.

ANKLE: Any deformity, discoloration, or swelling that leaves an ankle unable to bear weight should be treated as a fracture. Remove the shoe and make a careful inspection. If needed, the foot should be placed in the position of function with gentle traction. Secure the ankle and foot in this position, or as close to it as possible.

FOOT: Same as ankle.

TOES: These little bones are usually damaged by violent stubs or something heavy being dropped on the toe and crushing the bone. Tape the toe to a healthy neighbor with cotton or gauze between the toes. Stiff-soled boots may enable the patient to walk out, or even continue the trip.

Complicated Fractures

Angulations

It is difficult to splint the unnaturally aligned bone. The patient suffers from pain and anguish over the deformity. Adequate circulation may be cut off by the angulation. For these reasons it is best to attempt to replace the bone in a natural alignment. The method is traction-in-line and reduction. Pulling slowly, steadily and gently on the bone along the line in which it lies will relax the muscle, reduce the pain, and allow you to slowly move it gently into alignment. The sooner this attempt at reduction is made, the better. Do not continue if the patient complains of increasing pain. Do not continue if you have to use force to move it. Once aligned, splint as usual. If alignment cannot be achieved, splint as best you can.

Figure 11-8
Traction-in-line to realign an angulated fracture.

Open Fractures

An open fracture is indicated by an open wound over the broken bone. Bones may or may not protrude through the skin. Surgical intervention is often needed. After six to eight hours, the possibility of loss of function or loss of limb goes up dramatically. If no bones are visible, clean and dress the wound, and splint. If bones do show, and if you're close to a hospital, traction is not recommended since pulling the bone ends back under the skin increases the rate of infection. Rinsing the bone ends gently (not scrubbing), and covering them with a moist, sterile dressing is recommended. Splint as best you can and evacuate as soon as possible.

When the doctor is far away, however, exposed bone ends do better when they're returned to the inside of the body. An infected bone has a better chance of being saved than a bone that has died from lack of blood and exposure. Flush the exposed bones without touching them. Gentle traction usually pulls the bones back inside easily. Dress the wound and splint. Traction is also required on a fractured femur, even if the fracture is open.

Long-Term Fracture Care

Monitoring is the name of the game. Keep careful watch on the Circulation, Sensation and Motion (CSM) of the injured arm or leg after the splint is in place. Swelling can cut off circulation and require re-splinting. Time and the bouncing ride out on a litter can loosen a splint and require re-splinting. It is important to give patients the responsibility of letting you know if there are any changes in their condition.

The question of how fast to evacuate the fractured patient will depend on the situation and the severity of the injury. In all cases, a wise backcountry leader will have considered the possibilities beforehand. Ask yourself before leaving home: What can be done if such-and-such happens? What are our resources? Where is the closest aid, and how do we contact them? An extended carry is a very strenuous event even when you have a dozen people to switch off on the litter. And the patient's gear may have to be carried as well.

Fractures that should be evacuated soon include: 1) suspected spinal injuries, 2) pelvic injuries with suspected internal bleeding, 3) any open fracture, 4) a fractured femur or a high level of suspicion concerning one, and 5) any fracture with tremendous swelling and/or loss of circulation.

The Barehanded Principles
FRACTURES

1. LAF (Look, Ask and Feel) at the injury.

2. When in doubt, splint.

3. Splinting should include padding, something rigid, and should be long enough to incorporate the joints above and below a broken bone or the bones above and below an injured joint.

4. Avoid the void.

5. Angulations should be reduced with slow, steady, gentle traction-in-line with NO force and NO increase in pain.

6. Open fractures should be cleaned and dressed. Exposed bone ends should be pulled back inside the body in long-term care situations.

7. Maintain manual traction on a fractured femur until a mechanical traction device can be applied.

8. Monitor patients for changes in CSM, and keep track of their vital signs.

9. Evacuate.

Chapter 12
Dislocations

A period of melt-and-freeze temperatures had left the snowy surface hard, with just enough of a crust to hold weight a teasing moment before dropping the snowshoers through into softer, underlying whiteness. For additional support, everyone was using two ski poles. It could have been frustrating, but the day's weather was pleasant, the group was congenial, and spirits were high. The walk up the ridge went quickly.

On the descent the trip went even quicker for Deborah. Her lighter weight kept her from crunching through on an especially dense crust in an opening on the steep forested hillside. She skied away from the group on her snowshoes. Planting a pole instinctively to brake herself, she slipped to the end of her arm's reach, and levered her right shoulder out of joint. Deborah plopped into a sitting position with a look of surprise that altered rapidly into one of intense pain. She sat huddled in the snow with her right arm cradled in her left. She was aware of what happened to her. Her shoulder had been dislocated in the past.

It was a matter of moments before her friends had her lying back on a foamlite pad. Sitting in the snow beside her, a rescuer pulled gently on the arm on her injured side. The pull was in line with the way she held her arm. As the pressure on the pull was slowly increased, Deborah was encouraged to take deep breaths and relax her muscles.

With a soft and satisfying thump, the end of her upper arm bone rolled back into its socket. Her expression changed immediately to one of relief, and she released a long sigh.

Unzipping her parka about halfway, she placed her arm partially inside. The parka became a temporary sling. With the group sharing out her load, Deborah was able to snowshoe to the van, about two miles distant. A short visit to the hospital revealed nothing extraordinary in her shoulder. She went home with soreness but no serious damage.

Any joint of the body can come out of joint. The mechanism of injury can be indirect (the stuck ski pole levers out a shoulder, the high brace of the kayaker pries out a shoulder) or direct (a fall on a shoulder knocks it out). If the bones stay locked out of normal alignment, the injury is a dislocation (a dis-lock-action). Direct mechanisms tend to cause more damage to the joint because of the forces involved.

Assessment

As with any musculoskeletal injury, have a good LAF at the patient (see *Fractures*). *Look* for deformity, and asymmetry. A dislocated joint just doesn't look like the patient's normally aligned joints. Look for guarding. Patients tend to protect injured joints. *Ask* about pain. Dislocations are typically very painful. Ask about ability to move. A dislocation prevents the normal range of motion in the joint. *Feel* for a pain response and deformity. Sometimes a rescuer's hand will "see" things that the eyes have missed.

Look, Ask and Feel (LAF) for adequate circulation beyond the dislocation. The skin should look healthy in color. The patient should not complain of numbness or tingling. There should be a pulse beyond the dislocation. Loss of circulation is the major complication with a dislocation, and a cause for determined action.

Treatment

Work quickly but calmly. The sooner an attempt to relocate or reduce the angle of dislocation is made, the easier it will be for you and the patient. She will feel better, and her joint will receive an adequate blood supply, if the relocation is successful. You need to get the patient to relax as much as possible. Ask her to take deep breaths, and let all the tension go from the painful area. Have her lie down. Lightly touch the dislocation, reminding the patient where to concentrate her attempt to relax.

Be assured that if you work steadily and gently, the patient's condition will be made better, not worse. Fractures, blood vessel damage, and nerve impairment often associated with dislocations will be improved by a non-forceful relocation. And the evacuation will be easier and safer for everyone involved.

General treatment includes:
1) Place yourself comfortably in a position allowing you to pull gentle traction-in-line.
2) Take a firm grip on the arm (or leg), pulling in line with the way the patient is holding her extremity.
3) Pull steadily, increasing pull slowly without jerking.
4) Do not use force. Stop if pain increases.

If the dislocation does not relocate after you've pulled traction-in-line for a minute, gently move the extremity toward normal alignment. Maintain traction during the movement. What you're trying to do is manually relax the muscular spasms and encourage the bones into normal alignment. You can move the bones toward a more normal alignment as long as the patient does not complain of increasing pain, and you're not forcing movement. The muscles, tendons and ligaments "want" to be back where they belong. You're encouraging them to move back. The patient will tell you when relocation has occurred. Most relocated dislocations need RICE, immobilization (see *Splinting*), and ibuprofen for pain, until a physician can examine the injury.

Occasionally a dislocation will be severe enough to prevent relocation. You will have to splint the extremity in the position the patient is holding it. Make the splint as comfortable as possible. Evacuate the patient as soon as you can.

Specific Dislocations: Upper Body

MANDIBLE (jaw): After wrapping something soft and protective around your thumbs, reach gently into the patient's mouth, gripping the back molars. Pull down and forward until relocation occurs.

CERVICAL SPINE (neck): Any deformity or loss of motion in the neck qualifies the patient for treatment as a spinal cord injury (see *Spinal Cord Injury Management*).

SHOULDER: There are many ways to reduce a dislocated shoulder, but this simple tried-and-true method usually gets the desired results. Help the patient lie down, offering support to the arm on the injured side. Sit down at her shoulder. Ask her to put her hand on her head and let her arm drop gently to the ground. If she can do it, this motion often lets the shoulder go back in. If she can't put her hand on her head, or if the movement doesn't cause a relocation, provide gentle traction-in-line on the arm, pulling in the direction the elbow is pointing. With the elbow bent, slowly move the arm into a position approximately 90 degrees from the body. Moving toward normal alignment mimics the motion the arm of the patient would go through if she were going to throw a baseball. The strength of your pull should ease the patient's pain but not cause her to slide across the ground. Swinging the arm gently in small circles may be needed to stimulate reduction. Maintain the traction. It may take time to achieve the relocation of the joint. Once relocated, immobilize the shoulder with the arm in a sling, if possible. Secure the sling with swathes or a wide elastic wrap.

Figure 12-1a
Reduction of a dislocated shoulder.

Figure 12-1b
Reduction of a dislocated shoulder.

It is not a healthy idea for you to place one of your feet in the patient's armpit and pull aggressively on the arm. The abundant blood vessels and nerves of the armpit can easily be damaged.

ELBOW: Traction-in-line is best applied by two rescuers, one holding above the elbow and the other holding below, with the injured arm flexed. An elbow can be dislocated to the inside or outside, and may require side pressure to the joint as well as traction-in-line. Fractures are often associated with elbow dislocations, and relocation is often difficult. Whether or not the joint is relocated, sling and swathe the injured arm.

WRIST: Dislocated wrists are usually fractured. They should be placed in normal alignment and splinted.

FINGERS: Keep the finger partially flexed and pull on the end while actually pushing the dislocated joint back into place. This is safer and easier than just pulling. Pad between the injured finger and a healthy neighbor, and tape the two fingers together. Do not tape the finger straight, but in a manner that allows bending of the affected joint.

Dislocations of the base of the fingers, where they join the hand, are difficult to relocate, and often require surgery. Treatment may be limited to splinting the hand and evacuating the patient.

Specific Dislocations: Lower Body

HIP: This relocation requires two rescuers, and still may prove impossible. Large muscle masses are involved. With the patient on her back, one rescuer straddles her body and lifts the leg on the injured side at the knee to flexion of 90 degrees. The other rescuer pushes down firmly on the patient's pelvis. Whether reduction occurs or not, pad between the patient's legs, and tie the legs together. The evacuation will be a carry-out instead of a walk-out.

Fig 12-2
Method for attempting reduction of a dislocated hip.

KNEE: With gentle traction, move the leg to a normal alignment. Splint the injured leg securely with padding beneath the knee to keep it comfortably and slightly flexed, and carry the patient out.

PATELLA (kneecap): Apply gentle traction in order to straighten out the injured leg. Sometimes the kneecap will pop back into place when the leg is straightened. If not, push it back into place. This may require some gentle "force," but the patella is an unusual joint, and a gentle push is safely applied here. With a circular splint that leaves the kneecap free, the patient may be comfortable enough to hobble out using an improvised crutch.

ANKLE: Dislocated ankles are usually very unstable and easily realigned with traction. Picking up the injured foot by the toes and pulling gently on the heel usually works. Ankles are also highly susceptible to de-circulation, and every effort should be made to return the joint to normal alignment as soon as possible. Associated fractures are common. The patient will require carrying.

TOES: Same as fingers.

Long-Term Dislocation Care

Regular monitoring is required to ensure your patient maintains adequate circulation to the injured area. Check often for a pulse, normal skin color and sensations beyond the injured joint. Give the patient the responsibility of notifying you of changes in her or his condition. Cold packs and pain-killing medications may be used to give the patient relief.

Most dislocations should be evacuated for careful medical examination even if they relocate easily. There is always the chance of underlying damage that doesn't show up right away, especially with first-time dislocations. Exceptions would include fingers and toes, and chronic dislocations (repeat offenders) that the patient is able to use with reasonable comfort after the relocation.

The Barehanded Principles:
DISLOCATIONS

1. LAF (Look, Ask and Feel) at the injury.

    A. Look for deformity and asymmetry.

    B. Ask about pain and loss of ability to move.

    C. Feel for tenderness and deformity.

2. Encourage the patient to relax.

3. Place the patient comfortably on the ground.
4. Pull gentle traction-in-line on the dislocated bones.
5. Under traction, move the bones toward normal alignment.
6. Do not use force.
7. Stop if pain increases dramatically.
8. Whether you achieve relocation or not, RICE and splint the injured joint.
9. Monitor the patient for changes indicating loss of circulation.
10. Evacuate.

Chapter 13
Thermoregulation

Environmental emergencies are medical conditions that are induced when the human body is stressed by environmental factors beyond its normal limitations. In cases of extreme heat or cold, the thermoregulatory system can no longer maintain a proper core temperature and life-threatening situations may arise.

The cornerstone of understanding these emergencies is an appreciation of the thermoregulatory system of the human body, its limitations, and what happens when those limitations are exceeded.

As a species, we are warm-blooded animals, which means that we expend a great deal of energy simply maintaining a constant core temperature. The ability to maintain a consistent core temperature allows us to function in a variety of environmental conditions. This constant core temperature is maintained by our thermoregulatory system. If our core temperature begins to rise or fall, protective mechanisms react to return our temperature to normal.

The thermoregulatory center is located at the base of the brain in the brainstem. Although it constantly monitors the temperature of the blood as an indicator of our core temperature, the brainstem itself does not have the ability to adjust the core temperature. The affector organs that adjust the core temperature are the skin and the circulatory system.

With many important functions, the skin is the largest organ of the human body. One of its most important functions is the maintenance of a constant core temperature. Under the direction of the brain, the skin has the ability to lose excess heat if our core temperature begins to rise or to conserve heat if our core temperature begins to fall.

Of these two extremes, heat and cold, the human body is better adapted at dealing with the heat. Until relatively recent history, humans have resided primarily in tropical and subtropical locales, where it was easiest to survive and thrive. Because we evolved in a hot, tropical environment, it was essential that we develop a very efficient cooling system. With few exceptions, ours is one of the most effective and unique cooling systems for any animal species.

Also, as a result of evolving in a hot climate, a method to conserve heat was not a necessary development. Having less effective mechanisms for heat conservation, we are more predisposed to cold injury than heat injury.

In order to maintain a constant core temperature, the thermoregulatory center in the brainstem has to balance heat production against heat loss.

Heat Production

BASAL METABOLIC RATE: The basal metabolic rate (BMR) is the constant rate at which the human body consumes energy to drive chemical reactions and produce heat to maintain life at a constant core temperature. It is the BMR that maintains us at 98.6° F.

NUTRITION & HYDRATION: Food and water are the fuels that are burned to maintain the BMR.

EXERCISE: The activity of using muscles consumes energy and produces heat faster than normal, thus increasing the core temperature and requiring cooling mechanisms to be employed.

Heat Loss

CONDUCTION: Heat is lost from a warmer object to a colder object via conduction. The most extreme form of conductive heat loss is a warm body placed in cold water.

CONVECTION: Heat is lost directly into the air. The extreme form of convective heat loss is wind-chill. In this case the warm body has heated the air surrounding it, but that warm air is replaced by cold air blowing around it.

EVAPORATION: As water evaporates it requires energy to convert from a liquid to a gas. This is our most important cooling mechanism since it accounts for greater than 90% of our cooling efficiency.

RADIATION: Heat is given off by a warm object as infrared energy.

With these few principles in mind, let's look at how heat and cold can tax the resources of the human body, decreasing our ability to perform and possibly producing life-threatening emergencies.

Chapter 14
Heat

Blueberries were plentiful and ripe under the late July sun. John, Jan and David were looking forward to a hike in the mountains with berry-picking as an added bonus.

Saturday finally arrived and they managed to get off to an early start. The hike they were planning was approximately three miles long with a gain of elevation of 3,500 feet. It would take them to an exposed ridge covered with blueberry bushes. Since they had been on this trail before, they knew that there would not be any surface water. They each carried one full liter bottle. The day was spectacular—clear, warm and sunny with a gentle breeze higher up.

Reaching their destination by noon, they were all soaked with sweat from the exertion of the climb. They sat like bears among the blueberries, enjoying the water from their bottles and the taste of the ripe fruit. For several hours they simply nibbled and collected blueberries, reveling in the summer warmth and the surrounding beauty.

Towards mid-afternoon David started complaining of thirst and decided it was time to descend in search of more water. Normally it would have taken them about an hour to cover the three miles, but on this day it took several hours and required an unusual amount of effort and exertion for all three.

Once down, they simply sat next to the car exhausted. Both John and Jan felt slightly nauseous and light-headed. David, on the other hand, was beginning to act strange, slightly disoriented and very argumentative. He stated firmly that he was hot, tired and very thirsty. With that, they loaded up the car and headed out.

As they drove towards home David became more and more disoriented and combative. His skin was red and hot. He began to rant and appeared to be hallucinating. Appropriately, his companions decided to drive him to the local hospital emergency room where he was admitted to the intensive care unit.

Quick action on the part of his friends saved David's life, and this incident involves all three of the common heat-related emergencies: dehydration, heat exhaustion and heat stroke.

Dehydration

We assume that our thirst mechanism will protect us from dehydration, that if we become dehydrated it will tell us by causing intense thirst that will not diminish until we are properly hydrated. But this isn't always the case. It is possible to lose fluid so quickly that the normal thirst mechanism is overwhelmed or overridden.

The sources of fluid loss are respiration, perspiration, urination and defecation. The rate of loss from each of these will vary according to activity levels, air temperature, humidity and altitude.

RESPIRATION: With normal daily activities we lose approximately one to two liters of water via evaporation from the lungs. As we breathe, the air that we inhale is "conditioned"—it is warmed to 98.6° F and humidified to 100% humidity. This warm, moist air is then exhaled and the cycle starts over again. The combination of extreme cold temperatures and altitude can dramatically increase the rate of water loss through the lungs, up to one cup per hour or six liters in 24 hours.

PERSPIRATION: With normal daily activities we do not sweat very hard so the loss is minimal, about one to two liters per day. But with exertion in hot, dry weather, this can become extreme. During heavy exertion, we can lose one to three liters of water per hour, which can easily amount to 8-10 liters of fluid while exercising.

URINATION: One to two liters of fluid are lost daily via urination to clear waste products from the blood. The amount of urine produced will increase with overhydration and decrease with dehydration.

DEFECATION: The average daily loss of fluid through defecation is approximately 0.1 liter. This can increase dramatically with diarrhea to as much as 25 liters in a 24-hour period.

Through the activities of daily living, the average day's loss of fluid is four liters, which is generally replaced by the fluid we drink and the food we eat. But the amount of fluid required can be significantly increased by exercise, sweating, diarrhea, temperature or altitude. The most common cause of increased fluid loss is exercise and sweating.

John, Jan and David thought they were prepared with their one liter of water each. They did not appreciate the amount of fluid that they would lose from sweating or the effects that dehydration would have on them. By midafternoon, when David began to complain, they were already dehydrated and suffering the consequences.

The effects of even mild dehydration are decreased physical ability, fatigue, and impairment of judgment and thinking ability. These factors increased the difficulty of the hike out and could have led to a physical mishap or becoming lost.

Once down to the trailhead, they each displayed other heat-related problems in addition to dehydration, problems to which dehydration contributed. Jan and John appeared heat exhausted and David's illness progressed to heat stroke.

Heat Illness

In the process of hiking uphill, Jan, John and David all began to overheat from the exertion. As our body core temperature begins to rise, our thermoregulatory system engages the cooling mechanisms. The excess heat building up from muscle activity is absorbed by the blood. As the thermoregulatory center in the brainstem detects the increase in blood temperature, the brain causes the peripheral circulation, the vasculature of the skin, to dilate, or open up. This dilation of peripheral vasculature increases the blood flow to the skin where the blood can be cooled. At the same time, to further increase the rate of heat loss from the skin, the brain stimulates the sweat glands to produce sweat. The evaporation of sweat from the skin increases the rate of cooling many times.

Sweat consists primarily of water and some electrolytes, specifically sodium and chloride ions. As long as we can sweat and the sweat can evaporate, we can continue to cool ourselves efficiently. But if for some reason either the sweating mechanism begins to fail or the sweat cannot evaporate, then the cooling mechanism will fail.

On hot, very humid days our cooling mechanism is extremely inefficient, and it becomes relatively easy to overheat because the sweat cannot evaporate. The evaporation of sweat from skin accounts for 90% of our cooling ability. Additionally, our ability to sweat diminishes as we become dehydrated.

Heat Exhaustion

Jan and John both experienced heat exhaustion, a condition caused by water and electrolyte loss. The primary cause of symptoms appears to be related to the amount of sodium and chloride ions rather than the amount of water lost.

Heat exhaustion is not a life-threatening illness. Little or no rise in body core temperature will be noted. As with Jan and John, symptoms include fatigue, exhaustion, nausea, lightheadedness and possibly heat cramps. Heat exhaustion usually comes on several hours after exertion and dehydration. The individual may have even replaced the lost fluids but not the electrolytes.

With enough rest and water, heat exhaustion is self-correcting. However, this condition can often be treated rapidly with an electrolyte solution consisting of one teaspoon of salt (sodium chloride) dissolved in a liter of water, which should be slowly sipped over a period of 60 minutes. Add a tablespoon of sugar or a sweet drink powder to replenish energy stores. It's better if the water is cold.

Salt tablets are too concentrated and should be avoided. They draw water into the stomach to dilute the salt, while the sufferer needs the water out in the circulatory system where it is used to help maintain a normal core temperature.

HEAT CRAMPS, sometimes associated with heat exhaustion, are painful but not damaging to the patient unless the cramps are ignored and the sufferer pushes on. As with any cramp, they can be stretched and massaged away. Drinking slightly salty water and resting should keep them from reappearing. If they do reappear, the patient should take the rest of the day off.

Prevention

Heat exhaustion can be avoided by consuming enough water to replace the fluids lost, and eating salty foods or drinking an electrolyte solution. Drink because you know you should, not because you feel thirst (see *Common Simple Problems: Dehydration*). Keep yourself and your group at a pace that allows your body to adapt to the heat. If you feel the symptoms of exhaustion coming on, you're going too fast. It is especially important to pace yourself early in the hot, humid season. Your thermoregulatory system will become more efficient as it gets used to hot weather. Take a break during the hottest part of the day, the middle afternoon hours. Wear cotton clothing that lets air pass through and sweat evaporate. And wear a brimmed hat or cap to shade your heat-conscious head.

Heat Stroke

Heat stroke, on the other hand, is a life-threatening emergency. Without proper care, heat stroke victims will most likely die. David displayed the classic signs and symptoms of exertional heat stroke. David's situation was much more severe than his companions' because he began to produce heat faster than he could shed it, which caused his core temperature to rise to dangerous heights.

Once our cooling mechanism fails, our core temperature begins to rise rapidly. Death can occur in as little as 30 minutes. With the rising core temperature, the brain, which can only exist in a very narrow temperature range, begins to fail. In an effort to cool the blood and lower the core temperature, the brain will dilate all the blood vessels in the skin. As a result, the skin becomes RED and HOT, but may still be WET. (Note: Classical heat stroke, suffered more commonly by the ill and/or elderly, usually produces DRY skin from severe dehydration.)

As the brain overheats, the individual may become disoriented, combative, argumentative, and may hallucinate wildly. David exhibited all of these symptoms and was appropriately taken to the local emergency room. But heat stroke treatment should be begun immediately in the backcountry.

The primary goal of therapy is to cool the victim as rapidly as possible. Since the sweating mechanism has failed, we have to sweat for the patient. The simplest and most efficient method is to remove all non-cotton clothing and soak the victim with water, fanning to increase the rate of evaporation, and massaging extremities to encourage the return of cool blood to the core. With a limited supply of water, cooling the head and neck becomes the top priority. If available, ice packs should be placed at the neck, armpits and groin, in that order. All heat stroke victims must be transported to the hospital as quickly as possible, continuing the cooling process during evacuation.

Heat stroke victims are dehydrated and require rehydration. Unfortunately, getting the patient to drink may be impossible. With impaired mental condition, it is inappropriate to force fluids. Continue cooling externally in hopes the patient will recover enough to begin oral rehydration.

Prevention

Heat stroke, like all heat-related illnesses, is preventable. The same prevention methods that work for dehydration and exhaustion will work for heat stroke. The guiding principle is to stay well hydrated (see *Common Simple Problems: Dehydration & Water Disinfection*). Do not rely upon your thirst mechanism to tell you when and how much you need to drink. Under conditions of exertion, it is probably impossible to drink too much water.

The Barehanded Principles:

HEAT
1. Stay well hydrated and munch salty snacks.
2. Rest often out of the heat.
3. Wear clothing that allows evaporation, & a brimmed hat or cap.
4. Give heat exhausted patients lots of water with a teaspoon of salt per liter. And let them rest.
5. Cool heat stroke victims as rapidly as possible. Pour on water, fan, massage extremities. Evacuate patients.

Chapter 15
Cold

It had snowed in the higher elevations, creating a spectacular view of lightly dusted mountain tops. A magnificent sight greeted Peter and Alphonso as they crawled out of their sleeping beds into the crisp mountain air.

Anxious to get started, they had a quick breakfast of hot chocolate and bagels, packed up their gear, and were off to chase the snow line several thousand feet above them.

Both Peter and Alphonso had some experience in hiking and camping, but little experience in winter camping. What they lacked in experience they made up for in enthusiasm. Before long, they were stripped down to their T-shirts in an effort to stay cool while rushing uphill to reach the summit. An occasional stop to snack on cheese and bread and sip water served to add fuel to their internal fires and replace some of the fluid lost to sweat. Several hours later they found themselves above treeline, with a gentle cool breeze and a slightly overcast sky.

Now hiking in about six inches of snow, they estimated that they would summit by noon. Their pace slowed as the temperature dropped and the breeze changed to a cold wind. Alphonso was the first to suggest that they stop and put on some warmer clothing. As Alphonso put on a pile top and a windbreaker, Peter explained that he was not cold and the additional clothing would only cause him to start sweating again.

The hour to the summit turned into several. Finally, at about two o'clock in the afternoon, Peter and Alphonso reached the now cloud-shrouded top. They sat there on snow-covered rocks sipping their last bit of water, hoping to catch a glimpse of the valleys below.

After 30 minutes Alphonso suggested that they head down in order to make their car before nightfall. Peter, slowly getting up, complained that his feet were cold and started down, leaving his pack behind. Alphonso stopped him and had to assist Peter with putting his pack on.

On the way down Peter became very quiet. Occasionally stumbling at first, his walk slowly turned into a constant stagger. His speech became slurred, and he no longer made sense when he spoke. He seemed unaware of the cold, and began falling into the snow with regularity. Alphonso noticed that each time he helped Peter out of the snow and back to his feet, Peter made little or no effort to brush the snow from his clothing.

By nightfall they had reached their previous campsite. Peter was useless. Alphonso sat him under a tree and proceeded to set up their tent. With great effort he managed to get Peter into the tent and into a sleeping bag. Tired and hungry, Alphonso crawled into his bag for a fitful night's sleep. Come morning, Alphonso was unable to arouse Peter, and eventually decided his best course of action was to leave Peter in his sleeping bag and go for help.

Sixteen hours later the rescue team arrived to find an apparently lifeless Peter. Assuming the spark of life burned faintly, they treated Peter appropriately and evacuated him to the nearest hospital—an evacuation that took almost 12 hours—where Peter's treatment for severe hypothermia and frostbite continued. He was released 35 days from admission, leaving several toes behind.

Hypothermia

When a body loses heat to the environment faster than it can produce heat, the body's core temperature starts to drop—a condition called hypothermia.

The most susceptible organ in the human body to a lowered core temperature is the brain, which is designed to function optimally at approximately 98.6° F. If the temperature is elevated above or lowered below this ideal temperature, the brain will begin to malfunction. In the case of hypothermia, normal thought processes are the first thing to become impaired. Mild hypothermia could be termed "mild stupidity."

The increasing impairment of the brain, as the core temperature falls below normal, continues from the newest and most complex functions of the brain (judgment, abstract thought) to the oldest most rudimentary processes of life (movement):

98.6° F   Intact mental and physical functions.

96.0° F   Confusion.
          Apathy.

95.0° F   Shivering begins as a slight uncontrollable motor
          tremor.
          Loss of problem-solving ability.
          Decreased self-awareness and self-protection.
          Skin becomes pale and cool.

94.0° F   Occasional stumbling.
          Shivering continues and becomes an obvious shaking
          tremor.
          Little or no effort made to protect self.
          Little or no recognition of the present situation.

92.0° F   Difficulty walking/frequent stumbling.
          Shivering increases in intensity.
          No effort made to protect self.
          Speech becomes thick.
          Hallucinations may occur.
          Skin appears dusky gray and cold.

90.0° F   Walking impossible.
          Shivering is convulsive, coming in waves.
          Speech is very thick and difficult to understand.

86.0°F   Shivering activity has stopped.
          Pulse and respiration may appear to be absent.
          Skin is now cyanotic (blue).
          Body noticeably rigid from cold.

NOTE: Core temperatures are approximate and must be taken
        rectally to be considered of value. Taking rectal temperatures
        in the wilderness is impractical at best, and may dangerously
        expose an already cold patient at worst. Use obvious signs
        instead of rectal meaurements.

When the brain first senses that the body is losing heat faster than
the body is producing it, it stimulates the primary defense mechanism
against further heat loss—vasoconstriction of the peripheral circulation.
This vasoconstriction of the peripheral circulation occurs in the skin,
the affector organ of the thermoregulatory system, preventing blood
from reaching the surface of the skin where it will lose heat into the
surrounding environment. The lack of blood causes the skin to become
pale and cool.

If the core temperature continues to fall, the brain will stimulate the muscles to contract and relax or "shiver," a form of involuntary exercise designed to consume energy and produce heat without requiring voluntary work. As the core temperature continues to fall, the brain will increase the intensity of shivering in an effort to rewarm itself.

As long as victims are actively trying to rewarm themselves, they will shiver. For simplicity, shivering victims can be considered mildly to moderately hypothermic. As the temperature continues to drop, the shivering mechanism will not be able to produce enough heat to keep up with the heat loss, or the muscles will run out of fuel to burn to maintain the shivering. How long the defenses can hold up against the cold depends upon the rate of heat loss. When shivering stops, patients have lost the ability to rewarm themselves. If temperature loss continues, the profoundly hypothermic patient may grow rigid and appear to have no pulse or respirations, yet life may remain. Without help, death will surely be the result. This patient can be considered severely hypothermic.

Treatment of Hypothermia

1. For the mildly to moderately hypothermic victim, almost anything that helps them create and maintain heat will help: fluid replacement, food (especially simple carbohydrates), exercise, external heat sources (e.g. fire or snuggling with a normotherm). But remember to stay warm you must stay dry. Change wet clothing to dry. If you crawl into a sleeping bag with a hypothermic person, it's best to use zip-togther bags (to prevent crowding) and wear lightweight clothing (so your normothermic sweat doesn't dampen his or her hypothermic body). It takes time, but once mildly hypothermic patients have rewarmed, evacuation is not required.

2. If your victim is severely hypothermic, no longer actively generating heat, seek out or create a stable environment. This can be a tent, snow cave, bivouac shelter or cabin. Just as it is impossible to treat a burn victim in a burning building, it is impossible to treat a cold injury in a freezer.

3. Handle the patient gently. Rough physical movement can cause a victim's cold heart to stop. Carefully remove damp clothing. Assume clothing is damp. If victims remain wet or damp, they cannot be rewarmed.

4. Surround them with a hypothermia wrap.

A. First step: Insulate them from the cold ground with a sleeping pad and surround them with multiple layers of insulation. What you insulate them with does not matter as long is it is dry.

B. Second step: If possible, place warm water bottles or heat packs in their hands and/or at neck, armpits and groin, but do not place heat sources against cold naked skin—wrap them first in extra clothing.

C. Third step: Prevent convectional and radiational heat loss by wrapping them in anything windproof and waterproof.

D. Pay attention to details. It is absolutely essential that the victim be completely surrounded by all layers. Protect the head where heat loss can be extreme. The only thing exposed to the environment should be their face.

E. Do not expose the severely hypothermic patient to extremes of heat prior to hypothermia wrapping. Acid-rich blood from inadequate peripheral circulation can be driven suddenly to the heart with fatal results.

5. If they are conscious and able to swallow without fear of aspiration, give them a warm sweet liquid to sip. The shivering process consumes large amounts of energy. Muscles need sugar to shiver, and we need to replace the sugar being used up. If we do not keep adding logs to the fire, the fire will go out and the person will die. The hypothermia victim may not be able to digest solids but will be able to absorb liquids.

6. If the victim is unconscious or goes unconscious, do not attempt to give them anything by mouth. Hypothermia wrap them and seek help for evacuation as soon as possible.

7. Supplemental oxygen would be of great benefit to the unconscious hypothermia patient. If unavailable, mouth-to-mouth (or mouth-to-rescue mask) breathing may help keep a severely hypothermic patient alive.

Figure 15-1
Hypothermia wrap.

Hypothermia is probably the leading cause of backcountry emergencies, injuries and searches. The first and most important effect of hypothermia is that it impairs the level of judgment and blunts our natural protective instincts. As a result we become lost, unaware of the environment and changing weather patterns, and we take chances. To risk hypothermia is to risk injury in an unforgiving environment where help is not immediately available.

Prevention of Hypothermia

Understand hypothermia and our susceptibility to it.

Wear non-cotton clothing in layers, taking off outer layers before warming up and sweating, and adding them back on before cooling off.

Be aware of changing weather patterns. Put on your rain gear before it starts to rain.

Be aware of each other. Hypothermia occurs with little or no warning to the victim.

Eat often. You need fuel to burn to stay warm.

Drink often. Staying well-hydrated is even more important than staying well-fed.

Pace yourself and your group to avoid overexertion with resulting fatigue and loss of stored energy.

Know your limitations. Realize that we are not well adapted to the cold. We have to rely upon extra equipment and resources to survive.

Frostbite

Frostbite is localized tissue damage caused by the cold. It creates a spectrum of injuries depending on how cold the tissue becomes. Ranging from little or no damage to extensive damage resulting in tissue loss, this spectrum of injuries can be classified in three basic categories: frostnip, superficial frostbite and deep frostbite.

The initial stage of injury can be termed FROSTNIP, and it's not a true frostbite injury. Skin is pale and numb, cold to touch but still soft and pliable.

The first true frostbite is superficial frostbite. This occurs when the tissues are damaged by cold (ice crystal formation between cells and dehydration within cells) but without solid freezing of tissue. The signs and symptoms of superficial frostbite are similar to frostnip, pale skin and numbness, both due to decreased circulation to the area. Even though the area is pale and numb, it is still soft and pliable to the touch— it will dent when you push on it.

Treatment of frostnip and superficial frostbite consists of skin-to-skin rewarming. The cold area should be in contact with warm skin. For example, a cold finger can be cradled in a warm armpit, or cold feet placed against the warm belly of your backcountry partner. Do not massage cold tissue or place it near a heat source, both of which may increase damage.

When superficial frostbite is rewarmed, a large fluid-filled blister, sometimes called a BLEB, forms. If this occurs, do not pop the blister. Blebs filled with clear fluid do better in the end than blebs filled with blood fluid. But, no matter what fills the bleb, it is extremely important to insulate the area well with dry material to prevent refreezing. The patient should be evacuated.

If frostbite is not treated in the superficial state, it can progress to deep frostbite. Deep frostbite can be recognized because the affected area is frozen solid. This type of severe frostbite is extremely painful when rewarmed. Severely frostbitten feet, once rewarmed, typically prevent the patient from walking. Instead of rewarming, it is usually best to insulate the frozen tissue well to prevent any further freezing. It is also advisable to evacuate the victim. In extreme situations, when possible, deep frostbite may be rewarmed in the field. Rewarming should be rapid without being damaging. The best method involves soaking the frozen tissue suspended in circulating slightly-salty water pre-heated to 104-108° F. Too much heat should be carefully avoided. Once rewarming is accomplished, the affected parts should be gently dried, covered with an antimicrobial ointment, and kept elevated. Pain-killing drugs would benefit the patient. Refreezing must be avoided. Evacuation of the patient should be given priority consideration.

Prevention

As with hypothermia, frostbite is preventable. Unlike other mammals, we are not covered with a warm fur coat. Instead we have to carry it with us. The first rule in prevention of frostbite is to have the proper clothing for the environment we are going into and know how to use it. Ideal clothing will insulate well even when wet. It will not be constrictive, especially in the feet where humans are most susceptible to cold damage. There should be extra clothing available if we do get wet.

The second rule is to pay attention to your body. As soon as a cold or numb area is seen or felt, rewarm it to prevent superficial frostbite from becoming severe deep frostbite.

Stay well-hydrated, and eat often.

Immersion Foot

Immersion foot, or trenchfoot, is a common cold weather, non-freezing injury resulting from prolonged wetness that produces loss of circulation with tissue damage. Early signs of injury include cold, swollen, waxy feet, often mottled with dark burgundy to blue splotches usually on the underside of the foot. In later stages, feet become red and hot, and blisters often form. On rewarming, pain and itching are usual complaints. Field treatment includes keeping feet as warm and dry as possible, oral hydration, and ibuprofen for pain.

Prevention

1) Avoid tight-fitting and non-breathing footwear.

2) Change into dry socks at least once a day.

3) Maintain a regimen of periodic air-drying, elevation and massaging of feet (try for twice a day).

4) Avoid sleeping in wet socks.

The Barehanded Principles:
COLD

1. Stay well-hydrated: Dehydration increases the risk of all cold problems, as well as inducing fatigue and impairing mental abilities.

2. Hypothermia is the leading cause of backcountry accidents.
   A. Stay dry and carry rain gear.
   B. Eat often.
   C. Carry extra warm clothing.
   D. Watch the weather.
   E. Pace yourself and know your limitations.

3. To treat hypothermia:
   A. Get into a stable environment.
   B. Dry off the victim.
   C. Hypothermia wrap the victim.
   D. Feed a conscious victim a warm sweet liquid.
   E. Evacuate an unconscious victim gently as soon as possible.

4. To prevent frostbite:
   A. Stay well-hydrated.
   B. Use proper clothing for the conditions.
   C. Rewarm cold areas early with passive skin-to-skin contact.

5. If deep frostbite occurs:
   A. Do not attempt to field rewarm except in extreme conditions.
   B. Dry off and reinsulate the area to prevent further injury.
   C. Evacuate the patient.

Chapter 16
Lightning

It was a popular campsite, proven safe by years of unremarkable usage. The July storm, rolling in around 1:30 AM, brought heavy rain and booming claps of thunder. After a particularly close lightning strike, two leaders made a tent-by-tent check on their clients. As they moved toward the last tent, a scream sent them into high gear: "Susie's not breathing!"

Inside the tent, they found the 13-year-old girl not only breathless but also pulseless. They began CPR less than one minute after the initial yell for help. After several minutes of ventilations and compressions, Susie gasped for air spontaneously. The rescuers detected a faint pulse. For the next hour, she received periodic artificial respirations to supplement her weak breathing. Around 2:30 AM Susie started to move restlessly and blink her eyes. The storm beat fiercely at the camp for five more hours. The rescuers stayed close to the girl, monitoring her vital signs regularly.

During this time, other members of the group, who knew the area well, hiked out for help. Storm clouds made a helicopter evacuation impossible. Susie was packed in a litter and carried out at approximately 11:00 AM. Although the strength of her breathing and heartbeat diminished during the morning, and she lapsed back into a coma, she remained alive, and fully recovered after a three-week stay in the local hospital.

Electrophysiology
Lightning occurs most often on hot days when warm, moist air rises rapidly to great heights, forming dark clouds filled with static electricity. As a charge accumulates on the bottom of the cloud, an

opposite charge develops on the top of the cloud and on the ground below the cloud. When the difference between charges reaches a potential greater than the ability of the air to insulate, lightning reaches out to equalize the difference.

The bolt of electricity is a direct current that may reach 200 million volts and 300,000 amps, with a temperature of 8,000° C. The bolt may reach out over a mile in front of the storm, and move through a channel eight centimeters wide.

Lightning flashes out approximately eight million times per day worldwide, or 100 times per second. It can run inside the cloud, cloud-to-cloud, and ground-to-cloud. But the one that hurts people runs cloud-to-ground. Strikes cause more than 1,000 injuries to Americans every year. Between 100 and 300 of those injuries are usually fatal. Lightning kills more people in the U.S. every year than all other natural disasters combined, usually between May and September, and those who die are usually working or playing outdoors.

Mechanisms of Injury

DIRECT STRIKE: As the name implies, the bolt of lightning hits the victim directly. The victim has often been near or in contact with a metal object (bicycle, exterior-frame backpack, ice axe).

SPLASH OR SIDE FLASH: The lightning strikes something more appealing than the human (trees, shelters), but "splashes" through the air to hit the victim.

GROUND CURRENT: The charge radiates out from the strike point along the ground. This is lightning's most common way of harming people, and the effect may result in many injuries from one strike. Standing or walking with your feet spread creates a "stride potential," and encourages the charge to enter one leg and exit the other. This pathway spares the heart and brain but is not without hazard. The least damage done by a lightning strike occurs with the "flashover" effect, when the charge passes over or around the wet victim without entering the body.

BLAST EFFECT: The explosive expansion of air from the superheat of the lightning produces the thunder, and can produce injuries in a victim who is thrown by the sudden movement of the air.

Types of Injuries

CARDIAC INJURIES: The current of lightning upsets and sometimes stops the natural rhythm of the heart. If the heart is healthy, it often restarts on its own. But it may fail to start up again because it is too damaged or suffering lack of oxygen from . . .

RESPIRATORY INJURIES: The muscles used for breathing have been shut down by the charge of electricity.

NEUROLOGIC INJURIES: The victim is most often knocked unconscious by the charge, and some will suffer temporary paralysis, especially in the lower extremities. Seizures and/or the inability to remember what happened may result.

BURNS: It is not common to have serious skin and muscle burns after a lightning strike, but superficial burns are common. If the burn is deep and penetrating, the patient usually has much more to worry about than the burn. But treatment for lightning burns is the same as any burn treatment. (see *Burns*.)

BLAST INJURIES: The impact of the blast effect can cause just about any trauma you can imagine: fractures, head injury, spinal injury, dislocations, chest and abdominal injuries.

OTHER TRAUMA: Post-lightning strike victims complain most often of ringing in their ears, or loss of hearing, that usually resolves in hours to days without permanent damage. But deafness is not impossible. Ears may bleed. Temporary loss of sight is not unusual, but blindness is rare. Victims often are bothered by insignificant nausea and vomiting for a brief time.

Management

Two factors make treatment of lightning strike victims unique. One is the triage of multiple victims, and the other is the efficacy of CPR. In triage (the sorting of patients when a group has been injured), rescuers are taught to give priority to those still alive, and let the dead stay dead. It is the simple rule of "the greatest good for the greatest number." After a lightning strike, the still, silent victims are very often recoverable, and the moaning wounded can wait. Second, CPR done aggressively can bring many, many strike victims back to life since they are often physiologically sound, just "shorted out." So keep at it.

Otherwise, the basic principles apply. When the scene is safe, check the patient's ABC's. Humans do not store electrical charges, so they are safe to touch immediately. If the primary assessment is okay, go on to vital signs and the hands-on patient exam. Treat injuries as necessary. Evacuate lightning strike victims even when they seem perfectly well. Problems can show up days later.

Prevention

Avoid likely target areas. Does lightning strike in the same place twice? Yes, so avoid places that look like they've been hit before. Does lightning strike water? Yes, the most dangerous places are on or near large bodies of water. Move away from water during a storm. Does lightning like open areas? Yes, and it will strike the tallest object, which may be you, especially if you're wearing a backpack or riding a bike. Move away from tall objects and metal objects.

Currents of electricity run like currents of water, from high to low, so stay out of ravines and other low spots that collect water. Deep dry caves are safe, but stay away from the entrance where lightning may jump the opening where water drips. Shallow wet caves and overhangs are generally considered unsafe.

Learn to read weather. A developing storm tends to move very fast. When you see the flash, start counting—one one-thousand, two one-thousand and so on—until you hear the thunder. Sound travels at about one mile per five seconds. If you get to five one-thousand and hear the boom, you are one mile from the storm and well within range of the lightning. Seek a safe place before that happens.

Thick growths of small trees of uniform height are probably your best bet. Spread out the group to provide more safety, but make sure everybody can see somebody else. The lightning can't get everybody that way. Sit on your sleeping pad, or some other non-conductive object, and make yourself as small as possible. Huddled in a ball, keeping your feet close together, gives the least potential differences in the separate points of your body.

Figure 16-1
Position to reduce chance of lightning injury during a storm.

Unfortunately, there are no guarantees. Anecdotes indicate that the lightning will get you if it wants you. Be prepared for the worst.

The Barehanded Principles:
LIGHTNING

1. Avoid dangerous spots:
   A. Bodies of water.
   B. High and/or open places.
   C. Tall objects.
   D. Metal objects.
   E. Low and damp places.
2. Move to ground with a uniform cover (e.g. trees about the same height).
3. Spread out the group and make yourself small on an insulating layer.
4. If lightning strikes, give the still, silent victim priority treatment, and your best CPR, if needed.
5. Check victims carefully for other injuries.
6. Evacuate all lightning-strike patients.

Chapter 17
Drowning & Near-Drowning

The day was oppressively hot and moist, sultry, and the three high-school boys gave up on the fish and dove delightedly into their favorite hole, a cool hollow of water in the woods behind their houses. After the ritual splashing and dunking, two raced for shore. When they looked back, the third was gone.

About six body lengths from shore, turbulence in the still water caught their attention. Swimming back, they found their friend just below the surface, his foot caught in a tangle of submerged roots. They were able to free him and half-swim, half-drag him to shore. He was not breathing.

While one of the boys pedaled his bike furiously to the nearest phone to call for help, the other began mouth-to-mouth respiration. Within moments, the victim choked and vomited his lunch across the muddy beach. The ambulance arrived to find all three boys talking excitedly. The ambulance attendants had to convince the victim to go to the hospital for a check-up. He never returned home, dying three months later after a series of complicated lung infections.

In recent years, drowning has taken between 6,000 and 8,000 American lives every year, placing it third as a cause of accidental death. Death results from hypoxia, the lack of air under the water. A near-drowning is a submersion incident in which the victim survives the underwater experience for at least 24 hours, but does not necessarily go on to live a long, healthy life.

Drowning

Management principles don't change just because everybody is wet. Your first concern is safety, which means you must avoid turning yourself or someone else into a second victim in the rescue attempt. REACH to the struggling victim from a secure position. If you can't reach him, with arm or leg or anything extending your reach, THROW him something that floats. Or ROW or paddle out in a stable watercraft. To GO swimming to struggling drowning victims is to risk your life. Panic lends them great physical power and determination.

If the drowning victim has been knocked unconscious, attention should be given to the cervical spine, if possible. But not at the exclusion of Airway, Breathing and Circulation.

Those who die during the submersion go through a series of events that vary little from individual to individual. First, they struggle and fiercely hold their breath. Heart rates speed up and blood pressures rise. Second, the drive to breathe becomes overpowering and they suck in water. Third, water enters the lungs and begins crossing cell walls and entering the blood stream. Victims whose lungs are full of water are referred to as "wet" drownings, and they comprise 85-90% of the total drowned victims. (The other 10-15% have "dry" lungs due to a constriction of their throat muscles, a laryngospasm, which keeps the water out.) Fourth, water continues to enter their lungs and stomachs. They often vomit, and consciousness is lost as they stop trying to breathe. Fifth, their oxygen-starved brain begins to suffer. Sixth, their hearts stop, and clinical death occurs. Seventh, the point of irreversible brain damage is reached, biological death.

When the victim is pulled from the water, treatment must begin immediately. Mouth-to-mouth ventilation should start as soon as it is determined there is no breathing. Artificial breathing can even be done while the victim and rescuer are still in the water if the rescuer is stable (for instance, standing in shallows). A victim of laryngospasm will have an airway closed to rescue breathing attempts. If your rescue breaths won't go in, attempt to massage the throat, pushing gently but firmly along the windpipe in order to loosen the spasming muscles.

Once on the shore, determine if the victim's heart is beating. If it isn't, start CPR. Do not worry about water that may be in the lungs. The victim is dying from lack of air, and air must be breathed in. Fresh water submersions have a statistically better chance of survival because the fluid moves more rapidly from the lung to the bloodstream. Salt water may even draw fluid from the blood into the lungs. But rescuers can do nothing about the fluid. They can breathe vigorously for the victim.

Expect the patient to vomit. When he does, roll him immediately on his side, sweep out the vomitus, roll him back over, and continue CPR. Experts estimate six out of every seven drowned victims are pulled from the aquatic environment soon enough for CPR to be effective, if it is started immediately and kept up. It is sobering to consider the dead thousands, mostly children under 14, who could have been saved by trained bystanders.

The duration of the submersion event is obviously a factor in survivability. But the amount of time people can remain underwater and still recover is surprising. Especially if they are very young and the water is very cold. Humans, to differing degrees, may experience something that may be called "acute submersion hypothermia," which protects the vital organs for long periods of time, resulting in a resuscitatable victim even after prolonged submersions. In July of 1988, near Salt Lake City, Utah, a two-and-a-half-year-old girl was submerged for approximately 66 minutes in a frigid mountain creek. When found, CPR was started, and continued en route to the hospital. With surgical intervention, she had a 100% recovery!

Near-Drowning

In near-drowning, beware the shunting of blood from the periphery of the body, an aspect of hypothermia that mimics death. It may make pulses too weak to find. Starting chest compression on a cold but beating heart often causes it to stop. So take a much longer time than usual, a minute or more, to check for a pulse before beginning CPR on a cold submersion victim. Breathing for him won't hurt, even if he is doing it for himself already. Artificial respiration, therefore, should be begun right away if you think the patient is not breathing.

Near-drowners will probably be hypothermic, and should be treated accordingly. (see *Hypothermia*.)

Everyone who has almost drowned should be hurried to a medical facility as soon as possible. It takes very little water in the lungs to have profound effects on the patient. Vital body fluids are washed out, and unhealthy material in the water is absorbed into the body. Pneumonia, tears in weakened lung tissue, chemical imbalances in the blood, and other related problems may result in death days, weeks or months later.

Prevention

Once again, education is the key. Beware of swimming and diving in unsafe areas. Swim with someone who cares about you, and who knows CPR. Wear a personal flotation device (PFD), and insist on the same from those who accompany you on water-based trips. When crossing rivers on backcountry excursions, choose a safe ford with an open run-out in case you do fall in. Loosen your pack straps before crossing. You might need to shed your gear fast. The difference between an expert and a novice is attention to details.

The Barehanded Principles:
DROWNING & NEAR-DROWNING

1. If needed, start artificial respiration as soon as possible.

2. Safely remove the victim from the aquatic environment.

3. Once on a firm surface, start CPR when there is no pulse.

4. Watch the cervical spine, and do a patient exam for other injuries.

5. Avoid rough handling.

6. Treat for hypothermia.

7. Evacuate anyone who may have taken fluid into the lungs during a submersion.

Chapter 18
High Altitude Illness

A purple human lay stretched across the plaza at Tlamacas Lodge at 12,950 feet above sea level in Mexico. The day before he had been a British Caucasian in Mexico City, and the day before that a pale soldier in the United Kingdom. His pulse rate was 110, and his respiration was 24 and irregular. When we asked him if we could offer some assistance, he told us to "piss off" and vomited violently. We interpreted that as a "yes."

Exchanging pesos for a ride in a car, we took him down to Amecameca, 5,000 feet lower. He reported himself much improved the next day, thanked us profusely, and went to a movie.

The medical problems collectively referred to as "altitude illnesses" are the result of hypoxia, insufficient oxygen for normal tissue function. Those who become ill are those too rushed to acclimatize and those who are particularly susceptible. Untreated, the problems can lead to death.

Since there is a measurable increase in ventilation and decrease in aerobic exercise performance above 4,000 feet elevation, "high altitude" can be said to start at that point. But complications seldom occur below 10,000 feet, and rarely below 8,000 feet. To be safe, consider 8,000 to 12,000 feet as high altitude, 12,000 to 18,000 very high altitude, and 18,000+ as extreme high altitude.

The degree of hypoxia a climber at altitude experiences is relative to the barometric pressure. At 18,000 feet the barometer reads one half that of sea level, making the inspired pressure of oxygen also one half. You effectively get 50% less oxygen with each breath.

Acclimatization

Acclimatization is the process of adjusting to lessening barometric pressure. The rate of acclimatization differs with individual physiology, but most people will adjust enough to prevent illness if they spend two to three days in the 8,000-foot to 12,000-foot range, and not gain more than 1,000 feet of sleeping altitude each successive day. For instance, if you slept at 14,000 feet last night, you can climb beyond 15,000 the next day, but you should drop back down to no more than 15,000 to sleep.

The first stage of acclimatization, and our most important means of adjustment, is increasing our ventilation. Heavy breathing increases the oxygen content of the blood, thus getting more oxygen to body tissues. It is okay to pant. In the second stage, our heart rate speeds up. Our pulmonary circulation constricts to increase pressure in our arteries to compensate for the decreasing pressure outside. The blood vessels in our brains dilate. After five to seven days our heart rate returns to normal, but the circulatory changes remain. The third stage is a stimulation of bone marrow to produce more red blood cells, which increases the blood's oxygen-carrying capacity. The final stage occurs on a cellular level with capillary density increasing and muscle cells shrinking and mitochondria ncreasing. These cellular changes get more oxygen into action quicker and easier. Acclimatization is lost at approximately the same rate as it is gained.

Acute Mountain Sickness (AMS)

All altitude illnesses are degrees of the same inability to adjust, and result most often when a group fails to pace itself to the slowest acclimatizers. The most common and most mild form of altitude illness produces symptoms that can appear in as little as six hours after a rapid ascent to an altitude of 8,000 feet or more. Headache is the first complaint. Other symptoms include loss of appetite, nausea, lassitude and unusual fatigue. Vomiting may occur. Skin may become cyanotic (bluish to purplish).

Ataxia is a loss of muscular control leading to difficulty in maintaining balance. It is the single most useful sign indicating the patient is progressing from a mild to a severe form of Acute Mountain Sickness. A simple check for ataxia is called the "tandem walking test"—having a suspect walk a straight line touching the heel of the front boot to the toe of the back boot with each step. If he can't do it, he's ataxic.

Severe forms of altitude illness include High Altitude Pulmonary Edema (HAPE), the most common cause of death among high altitude climbers, and High Altitude Cerebral Edema (HACE). In addition to ataxia, the victim of HAPE develops crackles (gurgling sounds with breathing). Crackles are an indication of fluid (edema) in the lungs (pulmonary system). The sound appears most often in the right side of the chest, and without a stethoscope can sometimes be heard with an ear pressed against the chest wall of the patient. Chest pain, a productive cough, and extreme shortness of breath, even while resting, result. Fluid may build up to the point where the victim suffers respiratory and cardiac arrest.

In the case of HACE the fluid collects around the brain (cerebrum), and the result may be the sudden onset of a severe headache, hallucinations, seizures, unconsciousness, coma and death.

Some problems can mimic AMS: dehydration, hypothermia, exhaustion and carbon monoxide (CO) poisoning. Dehydration should respond to fluid intake, hypothermia to rewarming and fluids and food, exhaustion to rest and fluids and food, CO poisoning to fresh air and rest and fluids.

Treatment

Since you can't predict who will deteriorate from mild to severe altitude illness, and at this point the majority of life-threatening mistakes are made, a victim must stop ascending until the symptoms resolve. Painkillers for the headache, and anti-emetics (nausea-relievers), may be safely given. But the Important Rule is: Don't go up until the symptoms go down! In the presence of possible HAPE or HACE, the treatment is immediate descent.

In 24-48 hours a healthy person should acclimatize to a given altitude. The dead are almost always among those who broke the Important Rule.

Supplemental oxygen can relieve symptoms and save lives, but it does not replace going down. A common myth concerning bottled oxygen is that a little will do more harm than good. Any amount will help, but probably only for the time it is being used.

Acetazolamide (sometimes sold as Diamox), 125 milligrams twice per day, can stop AMS from growing worse, and often speeds the acclimatization process. It should be started early in the course of the illness. The drug, available in the United States by prescription only, works very effectively as a prevention, increasing breathing which increases arterial oxygen. Acetazolamide works especially well during sleep periods. It is also a diuretic, counteracting fluid retention. If you plan to use the drug as a preventive measure, do so with a doctor's advice—and stay well-hydrated.

If the signs include ataxia or an altered mental status, going down can be augmented with oral dexamethasone (often sold as Decadron).

The drug has shown itself to be effective in the treatment of severe problems and should be reserved for that purpose. There is no evidence that it helps acclimatization, but it may augment acetazolamide therapy for pulmonary edema. By prescription only, the recommended dosage is eight milligrams to start, followed by four milligrams every six hours.

All altitude illnesses may be treated safely and effectively with the use of a portable hyperbaric chamber called a Gamov Bag. Inside the bag, a patient experiences descent without descending, and relief of symptoms can be dramatic. Once again, Gamov Bag treatment should help a patient descend, not ascend.

Prevention

Prevention of Acute Mountain Sickness is best done by staging your ascent. Allowing adequate time for acclimatization increases your safety and enjoyment. Avoid a rapid ascent from sea level to 8,000 feet. Instead, spend a night somewhere in the 5,000-foot to 7,000-foot range. Once arriving at 8,000 feet to 10,000 feet, stay two days and two nights before ascending higher to sleep. When going higher, climb no faster than your ability to acclimatize.

Maintain a diet of 70% or greater carbohydrates, and drink enough water to keep your urine very light in color. Carry water and wear clothing appropriate for easy drinking and urination. Avoid respiratory depressants, like sleeping pills and alcohol, especially during the first two or three days.

Physical fitness does not protect you against AMS. Fitter persons are statistically more susceptible, probably because they tend to go up faster. Training is certainly healthy, but if the training is going to prepare you for altitude it has to be done at altitude.

The Barehanded Principles:
ALTITUDE ILLNESS

1.   GO DOWN.

2.   DESCEND.

3.   GET LOWER.

Chapter 19
Scuba Diving Injuries

Its use is so common many of us have forgotten the word is an acronym for Self-Contained Underwater Breathing Apparatus. SCUBA divers themselves have also become common, enjoying their sport somewhere in every state. What they don't enjoy are the medical problems that sometimes occur as a result of the changing air pressure relative to the depth of the dive.

Air pressure is defined as one atmosphere at sea level, and measured at 14.7 pounds per square inch (psi). The density of water produces rapid changes in air pressure as a diver descends. At 33 feet below the sea's surface, the pressure has increased to 29.4 psi, or two atmospheres. The rate of increase in pressure is constant, one atmosphere for every 33 feet descended.

Decompression Sickness

As the pressure increases, the amount of gas that can be dissolved in the blood and tissues of the diver increases proportionately. At two atmospheres, two times the oxygen and nitrogen from the bottled air the diver breathes will be distributed to the tissues of the body. Nitrogen cannot be metabolized, and builds up in the cells. On ascent, the gas is diffused out of tissue.

But problems can occur if the diver ascends too rapidly, or stays down too long. Bubbles of nitrogen can block blood flow and increase pressure on surrounding tissues. Decompression sickness usually starts within one hour following the dive, but it can develop up to 12 hours later.

Signs and symptoms may vary in decompression sickness. Pain is the most common complaint. Feeling weak and tired is also common. There may be difficulty breathing or terrific headaches. Death is rare, but paralysis may result from delayed treatment.

Decompression sickness is sometimes called the "bends." The pain is most often confined to joints in the arms and legs, especially the shoulder and elbow. *Bending* the joints increases the pain. Patients may complain of partial or complete numbness in their extremities.

Decompression sickness may involve the skin. A burning or itching is followed by blue and purple marbling. When these colors appear, the patient should be considered to be more serious.

If the sickness involves difficulty breathing and chest pain, the result may be death. If it leaves the diver seeming to have a spinal cord injury, the result may be paralysis.

Lung Expansion Injury

When the pressure on a gas is doubled, the amount of space it takes up is cut in half. When the pressure is decreased, the gas expands, and the expanding gas, inhaled from a diver's air tanks, must be allowed to escape from the diver's lungs on ascent. If the diver breathes normally while heading for the surface, there is no problem. But if the diver holds his breath, via forgetfulness or panicking, the expanding air may rupture the lungs. When compressed air is held in the lungs, these problems can occur from a depth of as little as four feet.

Torn lungs may produce a pneumothorax (see *Chest Injuries*). Large bubbles of air may enter the blood stream. Within minutes of ascent these bubbles can enter the brain and cause a stroke-like death. This is the most common cause of diving death. The bubbles may enter other places, and produce severe respiratory difficulties or cardiac failure.

Ear Barotrauma

Pressure-produced injury (barotrauma) from diving is most commonly experienced in the middle ear. Simply squeezing the nose and blowing gently keeps the pressure between middle ear and outer ear balanced for most divers. But sometimes it doesn't work, and the eardrum ruptures or the middle ear bleeds. The complaints are pain in the ear, and sometimes the jaw and neck, dizziness and nausea, and difficulty hearing.

Treatment

Ear injuries usually take care of themselves. Putting medication in the ear without a physician's advice is not a healthy idea since the eardrum may be open, but decongestant nasal sprays may help relieve the discomfort. If the problem is severe, have the ear checked. More dramatic treatment may be necessary.

Decompression sickness or lung injury require more immediate care. If the symptoms seem mild, place divers on their left side with their feet slightly elevated. This position helps keep bubbles out of their heart and brain. Giving them fluids to drink, and aspirin may help. Within a half-hour, they should be better. If they don't improve, or if the symptoms are severe, they should be on their way to a doctor, in the same position. Close monitoring is important. CPR may be required.

NOTE: Divers Alert Network (DAN) at Duke University in Durham, North Carolina, maintains a 24-hour telephone hotline for diving-related emergencies: (919) 684-8111.

The Barehanded Principles:
SCUBA DIVING INJURIES

1.   NEVER hold your breath while SCUBA diving.

2.   Keep injured divers in a stable left-side position.

3.   Give fluids and aspirin.

4.   Evacuate quickly to definitive care anyone not improving within a half-hour.

Chapter 20
Bites & Stings

The bites and stings humans receive from other animals vary greatly in severity depending on the type of animal, the reason for the attack, and the way the human acts during the confrontation. Despite the variations, similarities do exist in the damage done by bites and stings. And so we can find general principles for the management of the wounds received from wild creatures.

In order of significance, treatment for bites and stings should include 1) stopping serious blood loss, 2) immediate cleaning of the wound against the introduction of whatever micro-organisms were living in the mouth that bit or on the body part that stung, and 3) care to reduce the effects of envenomation if the animal was poisonous.

Reptiles
Pit Vipers
The scream came from behind a thick bush near Big Creek Trail in Idaho's Frank Church/River of No Return Wilderness. She leaped over the bush and several intervening boulders with surprising grace considering her pants were half down. The snake went the other way, even faster but with more dignity. During eight weeks of traversing a densely populated rattlesnake region our experience was almost always the same: we'd scream, and they'd slither away. The one exception was a couple of tense moments when a large rattler slid into a mini-box canyon in the middle of our path. It started back toward us before realizing the error and returning to the rocky corner in the trail. We gave it plenty of room while passing, and that was that.

Over the past few years, the number of venomous snakes attacking humans has averaged about 8,000 per year. Of those bitten, no less than nine and no more than 14 humans have died each year. The dead have almost always been children and elderly.

Ninety-nine out of every 100 poisonous snake bites are received from a pit viper (family *Crotalidæ*): rattlesnakes, copperheads, and water moccasins. The few remaining bites come from North America's only other venomous family, the coral snakes (family *Elapidæ*).

A pit viper's danger comes from two very special teeth, hinged to swing downward at a 90° angle from the upper jaw. The jaw opens very, very wide, allowing the venom to be ejected down canals within the fangs and into a prey's tissue. The amount of venom and the toxicity of the venom determine the danger to the bitten. For instance, the poison of the Mojave rattlesnake is approximately 44 times more potent than the southern copperhead's.

Pit viper venom is generally yellowish, odorless and slightly sweet to human taste buds. It evolved from the snake's saliva, which makes sense when you remember the purpose is to acquire and utilize food for the snake, not to deal death and destruction to large, inedible mammals who stumble over the low-lying reptiles. The venom attacks the nervous and circulatory systems of the snake's prey. In a mouse that can spell death in a few minutes. How dangerous is this venom to a human? Depends on the age, size, health and emotional stability of victims, whether or not they're allergic to the venom, where they were bitten (near vital organs being the most dangerous), how deep the fangs go, how upset the snake is, the species and size of the snake, and the first aid given to the victim. Arizona is the most likely place to die of a snakebite, with Florida, Georgia, Texas and Alabama filling out the top five.

One rattlesnake bite in four carries no venom. The other three will vary from insignificant to mild to moderate to severe envenomation. Mild envenomations hurt, swell, turn black and blue, and sometimes form a blister at the site. Moderate envenomations add swelling that moves up the arm or leg toward the heart, numbness, and swollen lymph nodes. A severe envenomation might add big jumps in pulse rates and breathing rates, profound swelling, blurred vision, headache, lightheadedness, sweating, and chills. Death is possible.

Coral Snakes
Venom from black and red-on-yellow coral snakes seems to be absorbed directly into the blood stream. Symptoms may come on very quickly, the pain changing rapidly to numbness. The bitten extremity

tends to swell very little. The victim may become drowsy, weak and nauseous, and progress to rapid pulse and respiration, convulsions and death from heart or respiratory failure.

Lizards

Only two lizards worldwide are considered venomous enough to end the life of a human. Unfortunately, meetings with both are possible in the Southwest. The Gila monster and the Mexican beaded lizard bite when they are picked up or stepped on. They have powerful jaws to compensate for primitive teeth and no means to inject the poison. They lock on while the venom drools into the wound. You may likely be required to heat the underside of their jaw with matches or a lighter to break their grip. There may be a great deal of local swelling and pain.

Treatment for Reptile Bites

1. Calm and reassure patients, putting them physically at rest with the bitten extremity immobilized and kept lower than the heart.

2. Remove rings, watches or anything else that might reduce the circulation if swelling occurs.

3. Wash the wound.

4. Measure the circumference of the extremity at the site of the bite and at a couple of sites between the bite and the heart, and monitor swelling.

5. Apply a wide elastic wrap starting above the wound and wrapping over and beyond the wound. This light constricting band should not restrict blood flow. Monitor the circulation beyond the band by checking pulse, skin color and sensations the patient may complain of (numbness or tingling). This treatment is controversial but unlikely to cause harm.

6. Evacuate patients by carrying, or going for help to carry them, or, if the patient is stable, by slow walking.

7. Safely attempt to identify the biting creature.

8. Do not cut and suck. Mechanical suction (not mouth suction) may be valuable if you get there in the first five minutes. Suction should be applied for 30 minutes via the Sawyer Extractor.

9. Do NOT give painkillers unless the patient is very stable, showing no signs of getting worse.

10. Do not apply ice or immerse the wound in cold water.

11. Do not give alcohol to drink.

12. Do not electrically shock the patient.

Prevention of Reptile Bites

1. Don't try to pick up or capture snakes or lizards.

2. Check places you intend to put your hands and feet before exposing your body part to a bite.

3. Gather firewood before dark, or do it carefully while using a flashlight.

4. Keep your tent zipped up tight at night.

5. Wear high, thick boots while traveling in snake country.

6. When passing a snake, stay out of striking range, which is about one-half its length.

7. If you hear the "buzz" of a rattler, freeze, find it with your eyes without moving your head, wait for it to relax the strike position, and back away slowly.

Figure 20-1
Black widow.

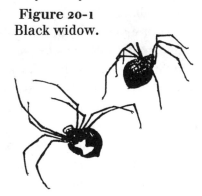

Arachnids
Black Widow Spiders

About 265,000 per acre! is the answer. How many spiders live in the same forested land we enjoy? is the question. They all love the night. They all have sharp hollow fangs. All but one family have venom glands. They are all strict carnivores.

But very, very few pose a serious threat to humans. One of those is black and beautiful, genus *Lactrodectus*, the shiny female black widow spider. She packs more danger in every drop of venom than any other creature in North America. Fortunately, she is small, reaching a body length usually no more than 18 millimeters, and more often smaller. Her drop of poison is tiny. The hourglass on her abdomen helps identify her.

She has been found in every state but Alaska, privately secluding her web under logs and pieces of bark, in stone crevices, deep in clumps of heavy vegetation. Rarely aggressive, she may be touchy during mating and egg-tending season.

You almost never feel the bite. There may be little or no redness and swelling at the site initially, but a small red bump may form later. Within 10-60 minutes symptoms begin to occur. Pain and anxiety become intense. Muscular cramping often spreads from the wound, settling in the abdomen and back. Burning or numbness characteristically disturb the victim's feet. Watch for headaches, nausea, vomiting, dizziness, heavy sweating—common reactions.

You might think you're going to die, but black widows kill only two to four people each year, and they are almost always the very young, the very old or the very allergic.

Keep the victim as calm as possible. That is your best first-aid treatment. If you can find the bite site, wash it and apply an antiseptic like povidone-iodine. Cooling the injury, with ice if possible, with water or wet compresses if necessary, will reduce the pain. Cold also reduces circulation, which slows down the spread of the venom.

Evacuation to a medical facility is a great idea, just in case complications arise. Most people will receive painkillers and eight to 12 hours of observation. Youngsters and oldsters may be admitted for 24 hours. Antivenin is available if needed.

Undisturbed black widows do not attack humans. Flies are her major source of food. She may consume 2,000 insects in her lifetime. Her value to the economy of life is great. Perhaps she deserves less fear and more respect.

Figure 20-2
Brown recluse.

Recluse (Fiddleback) Spiders

Her name, black widow, is the stuff of nightmares and legends, but the most common serious spider bite in the United States is not from her venom. Instead, look for the secretive recluse, genus *Loxosceles*. Generally pale brown to reddish, and nine millimeters to 14 millimeters in length, with long slender legs, they most often have the shape of a violin on the front portion of their body. The head of this "fiddle" points toward the tail of the spider. Unlike the black widow, both sexes of *Loxosceles* are dangerous.

The recluse prefers the dark and dry places of the South and southern Midwest, but travels comfortably in the freight of trucks and trains, and probably can be found in all fifty states. These spiders don't mind the company of humans, and set up web-keeping underneath furniture, within hanging curtains, and in the shadowed corners of closets. Their bite is more common indoors, but they live well-hidden beneath rocks, dead logs, and pieces of bark in forests all over America. They attack more readily in the warmer months, and curious children are their most frequent victims.

Like most spiders, their bite is often painless. Having relatively dull fangs, the serious wounds they inflict are usually on tender areas of the human anatomy. Within one to five hours, a painful red blister appears where the fangs did their damage. Watch for the development of a bluish circle around the blister, and a red, irritated circle beyond that. This is the characteristic "bull's-eye" lesion of the brown recluse. The victim may suffer chills, fever, a generalized weakness and a diffuse rash.

Sometimes the lesion resolves harmlessly over the next week or two. Sometimes it spreads irregularly as an enzyme in the spider's venom destroys the cells of the victim's skin and subcutaneous fat. This ulcerous tissue heals slowly and leaves a lasting scar. In a few children, death has occurred from severe complications in their circulatory system.

Without the spider as evidence, it is difficult to be sure what is causing the problem. Initially, there is little to be done other than calming the victim and applying cold to the site of the bite for reduction of pain. Any "volcanic" skin ulcers should be seen by a physician as soon as possible. Antibiotic therapy usually clears up the problem. Excision of the wound is sometimes required.

Scorpions

The campfire danced in a pit scooped out of the sand on the banks of the St. Johns River in northern Florida. It gave enough light to add ominously huge shadows to the small scorpion crawling up her arm. She, of course, swept it away. Then screamed in pain. We spent a panicky twenty minutes deciding what to do and then loading the canoe for an evacuation. Before the tent was down, her pain was gone with no ill effects.

Worldwide, mostly in warm deserts and semiarid grasslands, live about 650 species of scorpions. They all love the night and hide by day. They all sting with the tip of their "tail"—the last few segments of their abdomen. Their pincers are for holding and tearing apart their prey. Insects are their primary source of food.

Most victims report no more pain than a vicious bee sting. An attack of the species *centruroides* may be different. In North America only the *centruroides* is a known killer of humans. They are usually straw-yellow or yellow with dark longitudinal stripes, and reach from two centimeters to seven and a half centimeters in length. Their pincers are long and slender as opposed to bulky and lobster-like. The sting is immediately very painful, with the pain increased by a light tap on the site. But resulting deaths have almost exclusively been in small children, the elderly and the severely allergic. *Centruroides* is only found in Mexico and the southwestern United States.

First aid for any scorpion attack should involve cooling the wound, which allows the body to more easily break down the molecular structure of the venom. Cooling also reduces pain. Use ice or cool running water if available. On a warm night, a wet compress will help. And keep the victim calm and still. Panic and activity speed up the venom's spread.

If the scorpion was *centruroides*, post-sting manifestations may include heavy sweating, difficulty swallowing, blurred vision, loss of bowel control, jerky muscular reflexes, and respiratory distress. These serious signs are cause for quick evacuation to a medical facility. Antitoxins are available in areas where dangerous scorpions live.

In the Southwest, most stings occur May through August. The victims are usually putting on clothing, walking barefoot in the dark, or picking up objects like firewood off the ground. A bit of forethought can prevent most unfriendly encounters with scorpions.

Ticks

Unable to fly, hop or leap from overhanging limbs, it waits patiently at the tip of a tall stalk at the side of the trail. The wait might take months. At last, the backpacker brushes past. A relative of the spider, the tick crawls around on its unsuspecting host on eight tiny legs, looking for the right spot to settle down for a few days. It may search for hours. With specialized pincer-like organs, it digs a small wound in his host. Into the wound goes a feeding apparatus called a hypostome, and its relatively powerful sucking mechanism allows the tick to feed on the blood of the host. Anchored firmly in the wound, it feeds for two to five days, and drops off weighing hundreds of times more than when it first arrived. In the host it often leaves a reminder of his visit, disease-causing micro-organisms. Worldwide, only the mosquito spreads more illness than the tick.

Lyme Disease

Beware of the freckle that moves. The comma-sized *Ixodes dammini* tick is stirring up an epidemic of Lyme disease, and an epidemic of hysteria. First diagnosed in Lyme, Connecticut, the corkscrew-shaped bacteria, a spirochete carried by the tick, has spread to almost all states, still in heaviest concentrations in the Northeast and upper Midwest, and along the coast of northern California. The tick must be buried for approximately 48 hours in order to spread the disease.

Experts agree that the panic is unwarranted, but the disease can be scary. And it is the most common tick-borne illness in the United States.

THE WARNING SIGNS:

1) Two days to five weeks after the bite, a well-defined rash appears, a ragged bull's-eye, red surrounded by lighter shades. The rash appears anywhere it pleases, unrelated to the bite site, in several places at once, disappearing to reappear in different spots.

2) Flu-like symptoms, with a fever, headache, fatigue and a stiff neck occur before or after the rash. Rash and illness disappear in a few days to weeks.

3) Extreme, chronic fatigue with irregular heart beat and partial numbness or paralysis can occur weeks to months later in a few sufferers. This stage can be very serious.

4) Swelling and pain in joints, especially the knees, may start up to two years later. Any joint can be affected, and the arthritis may move from joint to joint with periods of remission.

Lyme is not fatal, although it is possible to die from cardiac complications associated with the disease. But without antibiotic treatment, it can lead to lifelong arthritic problems.

A blood test will show if you have the disease, but only in later stages. Early treatment is recommended based on symptoms if you have been traveling in a known *Ixodes* tick area.

Rocky Mountain Spotted Fever

Montana's Bitterroot Mountains first recorded RMSF, but it spread from coast to coast. After feeding for approximately three hours, infected ticks may pass the disease. Three to twelve days later, the patient develops a spotty rash, usually beginning on the hands, feet, wrists and ankles. The spots migrate over the arms, legs, face and abdomen. Severe headaches are common, with stiff neck and back, and general muscle aches. The characteristic fever rises during the first days and remains high. If untreated, approximately 20% of the victims will die. Almost everyone will recover with antibiotic treatment.

Colorado Tick Fever

All the Rocky Mountain states have had victims of CTF, as well as western Canada and South Dakota. A virus produces the sudden fever with muscle aches and headache that develops three to six days after the bite of the tick. Diarrhea, vomiting and stomachaches are common signs and symptoms. The patient often recovers and relapses several times in the course of the illness. It is very rarely fatal, although sufferers report feeling so crummy they wish they could die.

Tularemia

Another bacteria, often borne by ticks of the South and Southwest, causes the high fever and flu-like symptoms of tularemia. A decaying wound at the site of the bite is common. Antibiotics will defeat the bacteria.

Ticked Off

Quick tick removal is necessary to reduce the chance of disease transmission. Forget those ineffective and possibly dangerous ways of smearing them with petroleum jelly, nail polish or gasoline, or burning them out with a match. Using bare fingers to pull them out works, but it's not the best way. You can crush the tick, propelling its juices into you. A pair of tweezers should be in your first-aid kit. It the tweezers are fine-pointed, all the better. Grab the tick near your skin and pull out gently. A piece of your skin may harmlessly pull away with the tick. No twisting, yanking, or squeezing. Then wash the area thoroughly. Save the tick, preferably without touching it with your hand, if you would like to have it checked for disease. Make note of the time and your location to keep with the removed tick.

Repelling Thoughts
DEET (*n*, n-diethyltoluamide) still works when applied to your skin, but a new repellent keeps ticks from even finding life pleasant on your clothing. The ingredient is permethrin. Unlike DEET, permethrin is sprayed directly on clothing instead of skin. Apparently, it is not absorbed by skin, as DEET is.

DEET warning: Don't put it on infants and small children. Apply it sparingly. Don't use it repeatedly over long periods of time. Use lower concentrations—25-35% is enough. It is a proven carcinogen in lab tests.

Non-chemical means of tick avoidance are still useful. Wear long pants and shirts with long sleeves. Lighter colors make ticks easier to spot. Tuck pants into socks. Stay near the middle of established trails. Have someone check you carefully for ticks a couple of times each day on a backcountry trip or after any jaunt into known tick areas.

Rabies
Dawn brought a storm of unprecedented fury into an isolated Iranian village in the mid-1970s. Contact with the outside world was cut off. Driven by wind and floods of water, a pack of seven wolves from neighboring hills entered the village. At least 73 of the Iranians were significantly bitten, displaying obvious typical tearing canine wounds. Peace Corps volunteers treated the wounds but were helplessly without vaccination against rabies. All seven of the wolves were eventually killed, and all were tested positive for the rabies virus.

Of the 73 injured villagers, 30, or approximately 40%, developed rabies and died. The remainder, even though they received similar bites, failed to develop the virus.

From this, and other evidence, researchers have concluded that you have a four-in-10 chance of developing rabies if you are bitten by a rabid animal. This doesn't mean you should take the chance of not being treated. Rabies is a 100% fatal disease once the virus sets up housekeeping in a human brain. The only survivors of rabies are those few people who have received specific medication before the virus reached their medulla.

Annually in the U.S. about one million people are treated for animal bites, including those inflicted by other humans. Twenty thousand to 25,000 of these people will be treated for rabies. Each year somewhere between zero and three cases of human rabies will actually be diagnosed, and the diagnosis will be made postmortem (after death).

Statistics from the United States, Canada and Mexico give us the primary reservoirs of rabies. The major hosts are skunks (43%), followed by raccoons (28%), bats (14%), cattle (4.6%), cats (3%), and dogs (1.7%). The rest of the carriers were a few wolves, bobcats, coyotes, groundhogs, muskrats, weasels, woodchucks, foxes, horses and a rare human. The significant statistic for outdoor enthusiasts to note is 96% of the rabies in the United States is carried by wild animals.

Only mammals get rabies, and it acts in this way: The virus travels at a constant speed from the bite site to the spinal cord, and up the cord to the medulla where it replicates and demands the death sentence. It then travels back out along the nervous system. The animal becomes infectious after the rabies virus collects in the saliva glands. It is transmitted to other mammals through bites that tear the flesh. The incubation period in humans, the time from bite to brain, varies with individuals and with the bite site. Ten days is probably the minimum, and one year the maximum. An average individual would incubate the virus for about three weeks after a bite on the face, and about seven weeks after a bite on the foot.

Infected animals can spread the disease without biting. If their saliva contacts a mucous membrane (the inner surface of lips or the eye) or an already open wound, the disease may result. There are several well-documented cases of transmission by corneal transplant.

Rabies produces general early signs and symptoms: headache and fever, cough and sore throat, loss of appetite, fatigue, abdominal pain, nausea, vomiting, diarrhea. Once in the central nervous system the virus makes the victim anxious, irritable, depressed, disoriented, unable to sleep and prone to hallucinations. Victims may complain of stiff neck, double vision and visual sensitivity to light. You may notice muscle twitches and, later, seizures. The final stage includes bizarre behavior like aimless unreasonable activity, biting at those who approach, and drooling. Painful muscle spasms in the throat result when the victim tries to eat or drink. The pain leads to avoidance of swallowing, and thus drooling. Some victims will have throat spasms at the sight of water, and so the name "hydrophobia" (fear of water) became attached to rabies. As the nervous system deteriorates, victims become paralyzed, slip into a coma and die. Life after rabies is brief and very unpleasant.

Treatment

Immediate care for the bite of any animal, including rabid animals, needs to concentrate on cleaning the wound. Wash it vigorously with soap and water. Rinse the wound thoroughly. The sooner cleaning takes place, the better.

As soon as possible, have the wound checked by a physician. Tetanus or antibiotics may be recommended to prevent bacterial infections. The doctor might suggest you have the rabies vaccine. Fortunately the current Human Diploid Cell Vaccine against rabies works every time. A series of five relatively painless shots have replaced the old painful abdominal injections. To be most effective, the shots should be started within 72 hours of the bite.

When to be Treated

How do you decide if the animal whose bite you carry had rabies? There is only one sure way: Have the brain of the animal tested for presence of the virus. This is often impossible. Without the head, five other questions should be asked.

1) Was the animal one of the highly suspect species?

2) Was the attack provoked? Rabid animals tend to attack without provocation. For, example, trying to pick up or feed a wild animal and having it take a nip out of your finger is a very natural and unsuspect action. Having it leap from the shadows at your throat is an unprovoked and suspect attack.

3) If the animal was a pet, what is its vaccination status?

4) What is the geographical incidence of rabies in the area of the attack?

5) How did the animal behave in general? Loss of natural timidity and weird behavior are the surest non-clinical signs of rabies infection in animals.

When in doubt, get the expensive shots. If you make the wrong choice, you have accepted the death sentence.

Chapter 21
Bear Attacks

Dropped by helicopter in the Yukon-Tanara region of eastern Alaska, Cynthia began to gather rock samples as her job required. Minutes later she was surprised by a bear. Despite her yelling and backing away, the bear approached and suddenly attacked. Cynthia was thrown to the ground where she played dead. The bear continued its attack, severely biting her right shoulder, upper arm, head and neck. After several minutes of mauling, it dragged her downslope a short distance.

When the bear stopped for a rest, Cynthia, in an act of supreme self-control, keyed her radio and called quietly to the helicopter for help. Hearing her, the bear renewed the attack, removing all the muscle from her upper left arm.

Sensing the bear intended to eat her, Cynthia began to struggle as fiercely as she could, screaming and kicking at the bear. It backed off and moved to her backpack, tearing into her food. For approximately ten more minutes, she lay still and watched the bear. When the helicopter finally returned, the bear left the area. A brave and strong woman, Cynthia recovered, but her injuries required the removal of both her arms. The bear was never located. It had been a medium-sized black bear.

Encounters with Bears

Encounters with bears are always potentially dangerous. They are powerful meat-eaters, and we are weak meat. Although bears are unpredictable at best, historical evidence gives specific guidelines for reducing the risk of the encounters being harmful or fatal to humans.

1. Keeping your face toward the bear, back away slowly and quietly. Running makes you a high profile target that may attract the bear out of curiosity if nothing else.

2. Slowly loosen back straps and waist belts, in case you need to drop your backpack.

3. Look around slowly for trees that may be climbable, but keep in mind a hungry bear will climb a tree almost as fast as it runs.

4. When you have lost sight of the bear, move downwind and away while keeping an eye open for the bear.

5. If the bear charges, drop your pack and continue backing away slowly. It may be bluffing, or it may be distracted by the pack.

6. If the bear is a solitary black and it attacks, scream and fight back, using a weapon if possible.

7. If the bear has cubs, and/or if the bear is a grizzly, roll into a ball, pull your chin to your chest, clasp your hands behind your neck, make no sound, and play dead.

Prevention of Bear Encounters

1. In bear country, keep to wide trails or open country, avoiding a surprise meeting.

2. Make noise while you travel, especially sounds ranging from high to low, like singing and yelling. (Little dingling bells on your pack are of marginal use.)

3. Travel in a group. Bears rarely attack a group of four or more.

4. Avoid traveling in the dark.

5. Camp away from obvious bear signs (tracks, scat, scratches) and active game trails.

6. Loop a rope over a high limb and hoist your food above a bear's reach, or string a line between two trees and hoist the food from the center of the line. The general rule for bear-proofing food is: 12 feet from the tree, 12 feet off the ground, 200 feet to 300 feet from camp, and downwind. Consider toothpaste, deodorants, garbage or anything attractively fragrant as bear food.

7. Avoid smelly, greasy foods like bacon, sausage and fish.

8. Sleep in a tent, and bring nothing inside that might attract a bear.

9. Cook away from your tent. Keep your camp clean, hanging your trash with your food, washing cookware.

10. Leave your dog at home. Bears have been known to chase dogs back to their owners, and they arrive already upset.

11. Human sexual activity seems to attract bears . . . maybe.

12. Aerosol sprays containing capsicum, a derivative of red pepper, will often repel bears if you can give them a blast in the face—but the bear has to be mighty close.

13. Where permissible, it might be wise to carry a gun. It should be a big gun and it should be loaded for bear.

When the Bear Bites

Bears are capable of removing significant portions of a victim's body and leaving a high risk of infection. Of first priority is stopping bleeding. If rapid evacuation to medical attention is not available, scrub the wound clean with soap and water. Cover the wound with a sterile dressing, and immobilize the bitten area. Evacuate as speedily as possible.

Chapter 22
Dangerous Marine Life

Early morning, Christmas Day, 1984. The missing surfer, a loner, was found dead, his body rolling in the waves of an isolated northern California beach. He still wore what remained of his black neoprene wet suit. A bite wound extended from his left armpit to just above his left hip, twenty-eight inches across. Gone from his chest and abdominal cavities were the left side of his rib cage, his left lung, diaphragm, stomach, left kidney, and parts of his liver and intestines. Only one fish on Earth, said the experts from the Monterey Bay Aquarium, was capable of such a large bite—the great white shark. This one, they estimated, was twenty-two feet long, and weighed over one ton.

Below the dancing surface of the ocean, which covers about 71% of the Earth, live four-fifths of the world's organisms. Some of these creatures are potentially dangerous to humans. Generally, risky aquatic life can be divided into three categories: 1) those with big teeth, 2) those that envenomate, and 3) those that sting with nematocysts.

Those With Big Teeth

Of all fish worldwide, sharks elicit the greatest fear. And deservedly so. Their triangular teeth are continually migrating forward to fall out and be replaced by new ones growing in the back of their crescent-shaped mouths. The result is an orifice always full of razor-keen weapons capable of removing large amounts of tissue from a prey's body. They account for the most human deaths annually from aggressive marine life. Even so, the number of shark attacks each year averages only between 50 and 100 in all the seas of the Earth. It seems safe to go back in the water, considering the ratio of sharks to people who swim off shore.

If you work or play in the oceans of the United States, your chance of being shark food is perhaps one in five million. There are steps you can take to reduce the risk of attack even more: 1) Swim in groups. 2) Do not swim at dusk or during the night in infested waters. Those are the times sharks feed. 3) Wear bright or gaudy-colored swimsuits or wet suits that reduce the chance of being mistaken for something sharks like to eat. 4) Avoid turbid water where the shark's eyesight will be impaired. 5) Avoid thrashing and splashing and other erratic movement and noise that attract attention. Sharks hunt with vibration receptors as well as their eyes. 6) Be watchful if you are a successful spear fisher. Sharks also use their sense of smell, and are attracted to blood and other body fluids in the water.

If a shark seems interested in you, face it and swim away slowly. Avoid the crawl stroke, the butterfly, and other quick swimming styles. Stick to a breast stroke or easy side stroke. If the shark charges, curl into a ball. If it seems intent on taking a bite out of you, kick and punch at the eyes, nose, and gills.

In warmer waters, swimmers sometimes run the risk of toothy contact with barracudas or moray eels. Barracudas seldom attack humans, but when they do it is swift and fierce, and usually in murky water where they have become confused. Their big V-shaped mouths, with long pointed teeth, can do much damage. The glitter of shiny paraphernalia and jerky swimming movements may attract the barracuda. Moray eels do not bite unless threatened. Their sharp teeth and powerful jaws tend to hold a victim so strongly that the eel has to be killed to be removed. Divers are at risk if they stick their hands into coral holes and rock crevices where eels like to lurk in wait for more tastier morsels than humans.

Those That Envenomate

With the exception of sea snakes, venomous sea creatures are non-aggressive organisms that are stepped on or handled unknowingly. The most likely of these animals to become the victims of human carelessness are stingrays and sea urchins. Contact usually produces local burning pain, followed by redness, swelling and aching (and bleeding in the case of the stingray who has large barbs on the end of his tail).

The wound should be cleaned immediately with sea water. Explore the clean wound and remove any loose piece of the creature that may be stuck in the patient. Cleaning will also remove some of the venom, and, if the water is cold, relieve some of the initial pain. Scrubbing the wound with a povidone-iodine solution can help reduce the effects of the venom. As soon as possible, soak the wound in hot water. This may further remove venom and pain. Once the early pain has eased, the application of heat should not increase it. Check again for debris in the wound. These injuries carry a high risk of infection. When the wound has dried, cover it with a sterile dressing and bandage it loosely. With all marine-related cuts, a loose bandage is best, allowing the wound to drain. Monitor the patient for signs of infection, an indication a doctor is needed (see *Infection*).

Hawaii is the only state with sea snakes. Reptiles in every sense of the word, they breathe air but can remain submerged for hours. Commonly ranging from three to four feet in length, individual snakes have been measured to nine feet. They flatten out toward the rear, and propel themselves forward and backward with undulating motions, like delicate ribbons waving in sea currents. Attacks are rare, unless they are provoked. Their short fangs deliver a relatively mild bite. But the venom is very toxic.

Developing in minutes to hours, the patient complains of nausea and non-specific feelings of illness. Anxiety increases. Pain grows, with partial paralysis possible. Difficulty breathing may follow. Heavily envenomated patients develop a growing intensity of signs and symptoms, and may lapse into a coma. One in four victims die without antitoxin.

Treatment in the field consists of removing the patient from the water, and calming him or her down. Hysteria and movement increase the activity of the poison. Place a light constricting band, not a tourniquet, close to the bite between the wound and the patient's heart. Cutting and sucking is dangerous and non-productive. Evacuate the patient as soon as possible to a medical facility.

Those With Nematocysts

Coelenterates form an enormous phylum of sea creatures with around 9,000 named species—including all the jellyfish. Some of them are harmful to humans, with common names that sometimes reflect the risk they pose: fire coral, stinging medusa, Portuguese man-of-war, sea wasp, sea nettle, hairy stinger, stinging anemone. They all share a stinging organelle, called a nematocyst, that lives encapsulated in a cnidoblast on the tentacles of the coelenterate. The cnidoblast has a trap door (the operculum) with a trigger (the cnidocil) that opens the door. Filled with venom, the nematocyst has a sharp, coiled, thread-like appendage which springs out when the trigger is touched, lodging in the victim.

The reaction in humans will range from mild to severe. Mild reactions are immediate, and include stinging, burning, itching and sometimes local numbness to touch. The stung area may acquire a bruised appearance that lingers for days. A moderate reaction progresses to headache, nausea and vomiting. Severely reactive victims have difficulty breathing that may lead to loss of consciousness, convulsions, and the possibility of death.

Since the leading cause of death is drowning in the ensuing panic, removal of the victim from the aquatic environment is of immediate importance. Once safely out of the water, the irritated area of the victim's skin should be rinsed with sea water. Rinsing with fresh water may stimulate the nematocysts that have not fired to do so. Physically lift off any tentacles that still cling to the patient, but do so without touching the tentacles with a naked hand. The organelles that aren't rinsed off should be "fixed" so they will cease to envenomate. A wash of vinegar seems to work best. Alcohol, ammonia or urine have been used successfully. Meat tenderizer mixed with one of the liquids to form a paste and applied to the skin is an effective fixer. Keep the fixer on until the pain goes away. It might take as long as a half an hour.

The final step in treatment is to remove the embedded nematocysts. They can be rubbed off with sand and sea water, shaved off with a knife, or scraped off gently with anything that has an appropriate edge.

Persistent itching can be relieved with corticosteroid cream from the first-aid kit. The patient should be watched over the next 24 hours for signs of a severe allergic reaction. (See *Anaphylaxis*.)

Chapter 23
Medical Assessment

Little Jimmy stopped dipping his paddle uselessly into the Wekiva River and turned to me from the bow of the canoe.

"I can't do this any more," he groaned.

Knowing he hadn't been doing much of anything to move us toward our campsite for the last hour, I swallowed my impatience and asked, "Why not?"

Jimmy's reply was, "My kidneys hurt. I think they're failing."

One has a very short life expectancy, a couple of hours maybe, after one's kidneys fail! "How do you know it's your kidneys?"

"It happened last year about this time," said Jimmy.

"Tell me," I asked compassionately, "where it hurts."

Jimmy's trembling hand swept broadly over his entire lower torso. "Right here, in my kidneys."

I knew immediately that he was either lying, mistaken, or an anatomical marvel.

"Lie back against the cargo and give your kidneys a rest," I suggested. Every once in a while my medical astuteness amazes even me. By the time we reached our camp, Jimmy had made an astounding 100% recovery.

Sometimes the emergencies you face in the backcountry will not be caused by an injury, but by an illness (or by a supposed illness). The pain, discomfort, weakness, distress your patients feel will be the result of a non-injury variation from the way they normally function. Your job is to figure why they're dysfunctioning and how you can help them.

Assessment

Your primary concerns are still the same as with an injury: the ABC's. Checking and re-checking the VITAL SIGNS are still the important ways to tell how your patient is doing (see *Patient Assessment*). Your PATIENT EXAM may be revealing.

But the HISTORY you take during a PATIENT INTERVIEW will be the critical determining factor in your assessment. Consider the patient's answers to these questions:

Chief Complaint: "What hurts?"

Onset: "When did the problem begin? What were you doing when it began?"

Duration: "Has it been constant or intermittent?"

Frequency: "How often does it occur?"

Location: "Where is the problem?"

Radiation: "Does it radiate to anywhere else?"

Quality: "What does it feel like?"

Quantity: "On a scale of 1 to 10, how severe is the pain?"

Exacerbations: "Does anything make it worse?"

Remissions: "Does anything make it better?"

Prior History: "Have you had this problem before?" If so, what was the diagnosis, and how was it treated then, and are you currently being treated for this problem?"

Remember the SAMPLE questions: Do you have any other *Signs* or *Symptoms*? Are you *Allergic* to anything? If so, what happens? Are you currently taking any *Medications*? If so, what? Do you have any relevant *Past* Medical History? Any chronic diseases? Being treated for anything now? Any recent surgeries? When was your *Last* Meal? What did you eat or drink? What were the *Events* that led up to this problem?

Chapter 24
Allergic Reactions & Anaphylaxis

Summer! Once again the sun is high, and the days are long. For most outdoor adventurers this is a time when backcountry travel becomes simplified. You don't have to carry as much warm clothing or heavy winter equipment, nature is less hostile, and the perils of being in wild places seem non-existent. For a few, this is not the case. Instead, summer is associated with anxiety over an attack by a stinging insect, and the possibility of anaphylaxis.

Jan is one of those who worries. Last summer, Jan and her friend Mark were out on a week-long hike through a New England wilderness area. The weather was fine and the hiking spectacular. But in mid-afternoon of the fourth day, they stopped for a break and set their packs on a ground hornet's nest. Before they realized their mistake, both had been stung.

Mark and Jan had been stung before. Mark had the typical reaction: a painful, raised welt that cleared up over approximately 24 hours. Jan, on the other hand, knew that she was now in a life-threatening situation. She was allergic to the venom. When she had been exposed to proteins in the venom in the past, she developed a "hypersensitivity reaction" to them.

Jan ran down the trail to avoid more stings. Mark grabbed her pack and dug out the "bee sting kit" from a handy side pocket. Though some kits are spring loaded, Jan's requires a manual injection. Inside are a complete set of printed instructions (but they must be read before a crisis—no time for reading now!). Removing the rubber cover from the needle, Mark grasped the back of Jan's upper arm where it met her shoulder. He darted the needle in at a 45 degree angle, as far as it would go. Pulling back slightly on the plunger, he checked to see if blood was drawn into the syringe, indicating he had hit a vein. (If he hit a vein, he would withdraw the needle and insert it again.) He pushed down on the plunger as far as it would go. Withdrawing the needle, he massaged Jan's arm to speed the drug into circulation.

In moments, Jan could breathe easier. She took four antihistamine tablets that came in her kit. These usually take 30-40 minutes to be absorbed into the body. The epinephrine will last about 20-30 minutes. Occasionally the anaphylactic state will return before the tablets take effect. But Jan's kit had a second injection of epinephrine should she need it.

Within our bodies are a series of White Blood Cells (wbcs) that are constantly on the lookout for invaders. In order to do this, these cells must be able to distinguish between "self" and "non-self," so our own wbc's don't attack us. wbc's attack and destroy invading foreign protein. In the process they develop a "memory" of the invader so they can mobilize defense forces more quickly in the future. These additional forces are called in through the release of a chemical called histamine, released from our mast cells.

Normally, just enough histamine is released. Hypersensitive people release far too much histamine. Their immunological systems over-react. But why is this a threat to life?

Histamine not only helps call in reinforcements. It also causes itching and, perhaps, hives. Dangerously, it is a very powerful vasodilator, opening blood vessels up wide all over the body and producing the risk of shock. Histamine is an equally powerful bronchoconstrictor, causing airways to close down and causing the risk of inadequate breathing.

An anaphylactic reaction turns skin red within minutes, with a swollen face and tongue. Itchy hives develop. The patient experiences difficulty breathing, and it gets worse. Without immediate care, the airway may shut completely, and the patient will die of asphyxiation.

The best compound known that will reverse the effect of the histamine is epinephrine (adrenaline). It is available, by presciption only, in pre-loaded syringes. The EpiPen (Center Laboratories) is spring-powered and requires pressing the tip against the thigh or upper arm until the spring springs, and for 10 seconds more while the epinephrine flows into the patient. The Ana-Kit (Holister-Stier) is manually operated— dart in the needle and depress the plunger.

Anaphylaxis is not uncommon, and ground hornets are not the only danger. Almost anything eaten, injected into, absorbed by, or breathed in by a person can cause an allergic reaction. For simplicity, allergic reactions can be divided into two stages: mild and severe. Mild reactions are characterized by stuffy noses, itching, swelling and/or hives. They can be treated in the field with an antihistamine, diphenhydramine (sold often as Benadryl)—50 milligrams four times per day for adults—being a well-accepted choice.

People are often severely allergic to bees, wasps, yellow jackets, ants, black flies, and some foods and drugs. ANAPHYLAXIS is a TRUE EMERGENCY. As a result, hypersensitive people carry either an Ana Kit or an EpiPen (both sometimes called BEE STING KITS).

One concern often voiced is: Is it legal to give someone an injection? Yes, if it's their kit. But if it's your kit, and you recognize the inability to breathe indicating a severe anaphylactic reaction in someone else, err on the side of conservation of life. Leaders responsible for others in remote areas should consider carrying injectable epinephrine. In extreme cold, freezing should be prevented. Consult your physician.

The Barehanded Principles:
ANAPHYLAXIS

1. Before a backcountry trip starts, learn if any one of the group is hypersensitive to any known substances.

2. Carry an Ana-Kit or EpiPen, and know how to use it.

3. Ready the kit if a known hypersensitive contacts the allergen they are hypersensitive to.

4. Keep them calm.

5. Give them antihistamine tablets if they can swallow.

6. Give patients the injection when anaphylaxis is suspected and when they are wheezing or able to talk only in gasping one- and two-word sentences.

7. If the injection is given, evacuate the patient, even if she appears to be fully recovered.

8. During the evacuation, give the patient an antihistamine regularly (e.g. Benadryl 25-50 milligrams every six hours).

Chapter 25
Diabetes

Carbohydrates and some proteins are converted into glucose during digestion. Glucose is the main source of energy for the cells of the human body. Some parts of the body (muscles, fat, the liver) store glucose for future need. Some parts, especially the brain, cannot store glucose in significant amounts. To meet the needs of the brain, we carry sugar in our blood at all times. Islet cells of the pancreas form insulin, a hormone necessary for glucose to be utilized. Without it, blood sugar circulates but cannot be absorbed by cells. Diabetes is a disease characterized by a pancreas that produces an insufficient amount of insulin.

Sometimes the insufficiency of insulin production is complete, and patients must inject the hormone into their bodies on a daily basis. This is often referred to as Type I, or insulin-dependent diabetes. Sometimes the insufficiency is partial, and patients can control this disease with diet and exercise. They may require an oral medication to stimulate insulin production. This is referred to as Type II, or non-insulin-dependent diabetes. Patients with either type may be able to regulate their disease and lead an active life, traveling far into the backcountry. The diabetic who may need your care is one who is suffering from hypoglycemia (low blood sugar) or hyperglycemia (high blood sugar). Hypoglycemia, or insulin shock, is more common— and far more life-threatening.

Hypoglycemia
Blood sugar levels can drop to dangerously low levels in the diabetic who exercises too much, eats too little, or takes too much insulin. Because of the brain's dependency on glucose in the blood, hypoglycemia can quickly lead to unconsciousness, permanent brain damage and death.

The first sign is usually an altered level of consciousness, confusion, irritability and restlessness. Skin tends to be pale and sweaty. Pulse is rapid. Complaints of hunger, headache, dizziness and weakness are common. These signs and symptoms can mimic alcohol intoxication. The problem usually develops rapidly, and may lead to convulsions and coma. INSULIN SHOCK is a TRUE EMERGENCY.

If recognized soon, while she can still swallow, the patient needs a sugary liquid or another concentrated sweet source (maybe candy or syrup). Commercially made glucose preparations (e.g. *Glutose*) are advisable additions to the first-aid kit of anyone traveling with a diabetic.

As soon as the patient has regained a more stable level of consciousness, she should be given more solid food and encouraged to rest for several hours before continuing.

If the patient is unconscious, maintenance of the airway should take immediate precedence. Roll her into the recovery position, on her side, which allows for drainage of any fluids from the mouth while keeping the tongue forward and away from the airway. Rub syrup, honey, sugar or a high glucose concentrate from the first-aid kit into the cheek and gum and under the tongue where it will be absorbed by the membranes in the mouth. Keep at it until the patient recovers enough to take food. A patient who is slow to recover, or who fails to recover completely, should be evacuated for medical attention.

Any victim unconscious for unknown reasons should be considered a possible diabetic. Check quickly for medic alert tags or wallet cards. Question bystanders. Even without evidence, sugar can be administered safely.

Hyperglycemia

High blood sugar can result from too little exercise, too much food, or too little insulin. A diabetic who is sick for another reason may develop hyperglycemia due to changes in insulin requirements brought on by the other illness. Though not immediately dangerous, blood sugar levels creeping up over a period of days leads to increased urination as the kidneys work overtime expelling the excess sugar. Lost with the sugar are water and electrolytes, and dehydration commonly results. Untreated, the dehydration and inadequate energy supply can lead to impaired mental function, coma, and death.

The typical slow onset of this diabetic coma is characterized by growing irritability and confusion. Deep respiration (air hunger) with a fruity breath odor are common. The patient's skin becomes warm, dry, and flushed. Complaints of headache, intense thirst, nausea, stomachache, and the need to frequently urinate are common.

DIABETIC COMA is not common because patients usually notice the slow changes in their condition and take steps to reverse their deterioration. If they are taking the right steps and improvement does not result, they should be evacuated as soon as possible for insulin therapy.

Unconsciousness due to hyperglycemia requires a physician with all haste.

Sometimes you may not know if the unconscious diabetic is hypoglycemic or hyperglycemic. In that case treat hypoglycemia. Sugar may save the victim of insulin shock and it won't harm the victim of diabetic coma.

The Barehanded Principles:

DIABETES

1. Ensure an adequate diet with plenty of fluids is available for the diabetic before the backcountry trip begins.
2. Extra insulin should be carried in the backcountry, and not all of it in one pack or canoe in case of loss.
3. High and low temperatures can ruin insulin. Protect it from freezing by carrying it near your body. In heat, it might need to be carried in a temperature-controlled package such as a thermos or, much better, a Dia-Pak (Atwater Carey, Limited, Boulder, Colorado: (800) 359-1646; or a Medicool (Medicool, Incorporated, Torrance, California: (800) 433-2469.
4. As many people as possible should know the needs of the diabetic, where the insulin is kept, and how to administer it.
5. Encourage the diabetic to balance exercise ith food and insulin intake.
6. Diabetes affects the circulation of patients, putting them at high risk for infection from superficial wounds. Check regularly for small cuts and abrasions.
7. The same lack of circulation makes a diabetic prone to frostbite. Protect accordingly.
8. Any alteration in the level of consciousness of the diabetic should be investigated immediately.
9. Administer sugar for hypoglycemia, or if in doubt as to the cause of unconsciousness.
10. Evacuate anyone who does not show early signs of recovery.

Chapter 26
Poisoning

Any substance people eat, breathe, absorb, or get injected into their body can cause a malfunction in normal biological processes. The substance is then called a poison. Most of the deaths from poisoning occur in homes to small children. In the backcountry fatal poisonings are rare. When they do happen, it is usually the result of an inadequately ventilated tent or snow cave that lets carbon monoxide build up, the ingestion of a deadly plant or fungus, or injection of venom by a dangerous animal (see *Bites & Stings*). Giving the patient proper care requires you to first identify the problem, and second to identify the offending substance.

Inhalation

Stoves burn inefficiently in an enclosed space with inadequate oxygen. Higher altitudes increase the chance of poor combustion. The result of incomplete combustion is carbon monoxide (co). Carbon monoxide is invisible and odorless, and, once inhaled, it enters the blood of the victim where it is about 200 times more bondable to the hemoglobin. Hemoglobin normally carries oxygen out to the cells of the body. With co attached, hemoglobin is now useless. Tissue death can occur rapidly, and lead to the death of the organism (e.g. your tent partner).

As the amount of attached carbon monoxide increases, the patient's level of consciousness descends into irritability, impaired judgment and confusion. He will develop a terrible headache, loss of visual acuity, dizziness and nausea. It will be increasingly difficult for him to get a full breath, and he will grow drowsy. Toward the end, his skin may turn red, his heart will fail, and he will die.

Being careful of your own safety, move the patient to fresh air. If he has been exposed to low concentrations of co, he'll probably recover completely in a few hours. If the concentrations have been high, he may die even removed from the source of the gas. Rapid evacuation to a high pressure chamber and high concentrations of supplemental oxygen are necessary. Unconscious victims of co poisoning will need to have their airway maintained during the evacuation.

Ingestion

Swallowed poisons can disturb the body's balance in many, many different ways, and you may find it impossible to discover the cause of your patient's distress.

In general it would be a healthy idea to become very wary of any change in the level of consciousness of a suspected poison victim. Ask about nausea and vomiting, abdominal cramps, diarrhea, loss of visual acuity, muscle cramps or anything else unusual. Watch for signs of shock. Vital signs are important clues indicating the seriousness of the poisoning. The historical evidence you gather will be most helpful in assessing the problem. What has she put into her mouth in the last 24 hours? When did she do it? How much did she eat? If more than one person suffers, what have they consumed in common? If the patient is unconscious, what is lying around that could have poisoned her? Ask about underlying medical problems that could be simulating a poisoning.

If your level of suspicion is high, start treatment quickly. Each moment that passes lets more and more poison be absorbed into your patient's system. It would be nice to have a backcountry poison control center to call. The experts there could provide immediate and exact information to guide you. In their absence, you are left with some management principles.

If the patient is unconscious, try to carry out a sample of the poison. Evacuation to a medical facility is probably what is going to save the patient. Keep her on her side to maintain her airway.

If the patient is still conscious, limiting the absorption of the poison from the gastrointestinal tract is the prime goal of field management. There are two practical methods of doing this in the backcountry: 1) inducing vomiting and 2) binding the toxin with activated charcoal.

If vomiting can be induced early, within one hour, it may be very beneficial. Emetics are vomiting-inducers. A lightweight emetic for your first-aid kit is a small bottle of syrup of ipecac. An adult (about 10 years old or older) gets two tablespoons with eight to 16 ounces of water.

Younger people get one tablespoon with the same amount of water. Do not sit facing them. The vomit tends to come suddenly and forcefully, and may repeat several times. If they haven't vomited in 20 minutes, repeat the dose.

Without ipecac, stimulation of the gag reflex may work to induce vomiting. Lean the patient forward, reach into their mouth with a couple of fingers, and tickle the back of their throat.Do not induce vomiting if:

1. Patient is losing consciousness.
2. Patient has a seizure disorder or heart problems.
3. Patient has swallowed corrosive acids or bases which can increase damage asthey come up.
4. Patient has swallowed petroleum products which can cause serious pneumonia if even a small amount is breathed into the lungs.

For ingestion of corrosive chemicals or petroleum products, get the patient to drink a liter bottle of water or milk. Diluting the poison can reduce its effects. It is unlikely you'll be carrying many chemicals in the backcountry. If someone takes an accidental swallow of gas you bought for the stove, it can usually be easily managed with dilution. But don't let him smoke for a couple of hours.

Activated charcoal is post-combustion carbon residue treated to increase absorbency. For most poison victims, even if your care will be short-term, binding the toxins with charcoal is a better treatment than inducing vomiting. By the time you realize you have a poisoned victim, much of the toxin has already passed out of the stomach, and there are no contraindications for the use of activated charcoal. Charcoal may also be administered post-vomiting. The usual dose is 50-100 grams for adults, 20-50 grams for children. Although it is odorless and tasteless, swallowing the slurry of fine black powder may prove a chore. It can be added to flavored drinks (e.g. fruit drinks), but it should not be mixed with milk or milk products.

The Barehanded Principles:

POISONING

1. If the patient inhaled a poison, remove him from the source. Unless he recovers completely and soon, evacuate.
2. If he ingested a poison, find out what, when and how much.
3. For ingested poisons, administer activated charcoal as soon as possible.
4. Evacuate anyone who does not show signs of improvement quickly.

Chapter 27
Seizures

Suddenly, there is a great discharge of nervous activity in the cerebral cortex, the "peach pit" part of the brain. There is an episode of involuntary behavior, which may or may not be associated with an altered mental state. Your patient has had a seizure (sometimes called a convulsion).

It could have been a partial seizure, sometimes called a petit mal or localized seizure. A specific location in the brain is involved, and the patient loses contact with reality for a minute or two, and sometimes can be observed to manifest a localized motor movement. The partial seizure may or may not become a generalized, or grand mal, seizure. The generalized seizure can be shocking to watch. Patients grow rigid, and collapse into violent jerky motions. They often stop breathing and turn blue. They often are incontinent, and may bite their tongue.

Although sufferers are commonly referred to as epileptics when the source of the seizures is unknown, the problem may be caused by head injury, heat stroke, diabetes, fever, brain tumor, infection, alcohol or drug withdrawal, and assorted other overstimulations of the brain. Diagnosed patients often take drugs to suppress seizures (e.g. Dilantin). The overstimulation of backcountry ventures has been known to encourage seizures, even in people taking preventive drugs.

Frequent sufferers often experience an "aura," a warning signal telling them a seizure is imminent, and seek a safe place to lie down. A seizure must run its course—usually less than two minutes—once it has begun. You can't stop it, but you can protect the victim during the episode. Do not restrain the victim. Move objects away that might cause damage if hit. Cushion under the head with a shirt or parka. The patient cannot swallow his or her tongue. Do not try to put anything into the mouth. Many seizure sufferers are harmed by misdirected aid.

If consciousness does not return immediately after the event, roll the patient gently into a stable side position to maintain an adequate airway.

Take some notes on what happened: time, focal areas if you noticed any, length of seizure, triggering events if known.

Stay calm and comfort the patient once a normal level of consciousness returns. Protect the patient's dignity. Allow time and privacy for changing of clothes, etc., if required. He or she may not be sure what has happened. Don't let the patient drink or move around at first. Most patients will be in a sleepy-recovery phase after the seizure, sometimes called a post-ictal state. Check for injuries that could have occurred.

The greatest danger to a seizure victim is *status epilepticus,* a persistent seizure or series of seizures with no time for adequate breathing, and a TRUE EMERGENCY. If this goes on for too long, permanent damage or death may result. There is little or nothing to be done in the backcountry for this person.

Known seizure patients do not need to be immediately evacuated, as long as they are dealing with the situation, and their intended pursuits do not jeopardize their lives. First-time seizures, or seizures for unknown reasons, should be evacuated as soon as possible for medical attention. Once a seizure has occurred, thoughtful consideration should be given to continuation of the backcountry trip.

The Barehanded Principles:

SEIZURES

1. Be aware of seizure sufferers, and, if possible, their triggering mechanisms.
2. Make sure they are carrying and taking their anti-convulsant medications.
3. If a seizure occurs, protect them from harm.
4. Do not restrain them.
5. Do not put anything in their mouth.
6. Protect their dignity.
7. Keep them at rest and give them nothing to drink until their level of consciousness returns to normal.
8. Maintain an adequate airway for those who do not return immediately to consciousess.
9. Check for injuries.
10. Evacuate first-time seizures, and seizures with unknown sources.

Chapter 28
Heart Attack

Heart attacks still lead to more deaths than any other cause in the United States, and outdoor enthusiasm does not provide immunity. Coronary arteries, the vessels supplying blood to the heart muscle, are very susceptible to atherosclerosis, gradual clogging from fatty deposits. Encouragement for clogging comes from dietary saturated fat and cholesterol, cigarette smoking, lack of exercise, high blood pressure, heredity and aging. Atherosclerosis is a very prevalent form of coronary artery disease, and it precedes heart attacks.

Coronary artery disease shows up in three common ways:

1) ANGINA, caused by interruptions in adequate blood flow to the heart muscles, usually comes on with physical or emotional stress. The patient complains of chest pain and/or chest tightness. With rest and/or nitroglycerin, the pain goes away, leaving no permanent damage. Angina often precedes a heart attack.

2) HEART ATTACK (a myocardial infarction) results when a clot blocks a narrowed coronary artery, causing the permanent death of the heart muscle cells fed by that artery. Patients complain of center-chest discomfort: crushing, squeezing pain or heavy pressure. Pain may radiate to the shoulder, down the arm, and/or into the jaw, predominantly on the left side. Pain may wax and wane, but it does not go away. Nausea, sweating and shortness of breath are common. Patients often deny the possibilitythat this could be "the big one"— a heart attack.

In the backcountry there is little to be done other than keeping the patient physically and emotionally calm, in a position of comfort, and warm. They would do well to have a high flow of supplemental oxygen, which is rarely available in the wild outdoors. Do all you can to help maintain an open airway for the patient. If the patient has been prescribed nitroglycerin, make sure they've taken the pills as they've been instructed. Help needs to be sought.

3) SUDDEN CARDIAC DEATH.

The Barehanded Principles:
HEART ATTACK

1. Stay calm, and keep the patient as calm, warm and comfortable as possible.

2. Maintain the patient's airway.

3. Call or go for help.

4. Know CPR.

Chapter 29
Respiratory Emergencies

Few, if any, medical emergencies cause the patient, and rescuers, more distress than difficulty breathing. Although respiratory problems can have many sources, two are commonly encountered in the backcountry.

Asthma

Asthma is a recurring allergic disease that causes swelling, increased mucus production, and spasms of the lower airway. In addition to common allergens, attacks may be triggered by cold air, exercise and emotional stress. Patients suffer moderate to severe respiratory difficulty during attacks that may require your intervention. Air is often trapped in the lungs, causing the patient to breathe out slowly with difficulty and a wheezing sound. Treatment includes calm encouragement for the patient to relax and breathe with control. Pursed-lip breathing (breathing out against pursed lips) often helps the expiratory phase. Asthmatics should carry inhalers at all times, and extras on extended backcountry expeditions. Assistance with the inhaler may be required. The medication in the inhaler must be sucked deep into the lungs to work. In extreme cases, injected epinephrine in an EpiPen or Ana-Kit may open the blocked airway of an asthmatic. It should be injected when severe asthma is supected, and when the patient is able to speak only in gasping one- and two-word sentences. When the patient can swallow easily, drinking lots of water should be encouraged.

Hyperventilation Syndrome

Far from home, pain and fear often cause the patient to breathe faster and more deeply than normal. This hyperventilation may lead to chest tightness, lightheadedness, tingling or numbness in the hands, feet and/or face, and spasms in the hands and feet (carpopedal spasms), which lead to more fear, which leads to more hyperventilation. The patient will either calm down or pass out. If he passes out, he may stop breathing for what seems like a very long time—perhaps 30 seconds. Except in rare circumstances, the patient will indeed start breathing again. (If he doesn't, give him a painful stimulus. If that doesn't work, try a few mouth-to-mouth breaths.) Hyperventilating patients need to be calmed and encouraged to breath normally. When calmness returns, then you can investigate the cause of the pain or fear.

The Barehanded Principles:

RESPIRATORY EMERGENCIES

1. Stay calm, and calm the patient as much as possible.

2. Encourage the patient to breath normally.

3. If someone may require medication, make sure a sufficient supply is being carried before leaving home.

4. If medication is being carried, know where it is and how to use it.

Chapter 30
Gender Specific Problems

Injuries and illnesses related to the genitalia can be embarrassing, frightening, and sometimes life-threatening. These types of problems occur occasionally on backcountry trips.

For Women

Alterations in normal mentrual cycles are not unusual for women in the outdoors. Unsual abdominal pain, however, associated with abnormal vaginal bleeding should be reported to a physician as soon as possible. Pelvic pain with fever and chills, nausea and vomiting, and perhaps a watery, foul-smelling vaginal discharge also requires a physician's attention.

VAGINAL INFECTION: Signs and symptoms include excessive or malodorous vaginal discharge with redness, itching and, perhaps, a burning sensation during urination. Women with a history of vaginal infections should carry appropriate medications (e.g. Gyne-Lotrimin or Monistat). If the medications don't provide relief within 48 hours, the patient should see a doctor. In extreme circumstances, the patient may consider a douche with plain disinfected water or with a solution of two tablespoons of vinegar in a liter of warm disinfected water. A douche can also be made from two tablespoons of povidone-iodine solution in a liter of water.

Preventing Vaginal Infections:

1. Stay well-hydrated.
2. Decrease sugar intake.

3. Wear cotton underwear and loose-fitting pants.
4. Wash perineal area daily.
5. Change tampons regularly.
6. Decrease stress.

URINARY TRACT INFECTION: Signs and symptoms include increased frequency and urgencyof urination, often with a burning sensation upon urination. Low abdominal pain is common. Blood or pus may appear in the urine. The patient should drink lots of water and avoid sugary foods and foods that irritate the bladder (e.g. caffeine, alcohol, peppery foods). The perineal area should be washed daily with water and mild soap. On extended trips, women should consider carrying an antibiotic for UTI. Ciprofloxacin (sold as Cipro)—500 milligrams twice a day for seven days—is often prescribed. Consult your physician. (Note: Men are not immune to UTI.)

For Men
EPIDIDYMITIS: An inflammation of the epididymis, this problem tends to come on slowly, possibly with a fever, and is marked by a red, swollen, painful scrotum. The patient suffers, and the only immediate relief is found in rest, support for the scrotum (e.g. jockstrap, or improvised support from a triangular bandage), and painkillers. Antibiotics are necessary. Evacuate the patient to a physician.

TORSION of the TESTIS: TOT is a twisting of the testis within the scrotum. Pain tends to come on rather suddenly. Scrotum is red, swollen and painful. The lack of blood supply means death for the testis in about 24 hours. Evacuate the patient. Cool compresses and painkillers provide some relief. A jockstrap or improvised support may give some more relief and may increase blood flow to the testis.

INGUINAL HERNIA: When a part of the intestine protrudes into the groin or scrotum, the resulting lump and sharp, steady pain is called an inguinal hernia. Many sources of increased intra-abdominal pressure can cause the problem: lifting a heavy object, coughing, aging, trauma, weak muscles due to congenital malformations. If the hernia becomes stuck, twised or swollen, the intestine may become blocked, leading to potentially serious abdominal complications including a gangrenous bowel.

Attempt to reduce the hernia by having the patient lie on his back, head lower than abdomen, and applying steady, moderate pressure on the hernia. If it won't reduce, or if it reduces and later reappears, evacuate the patient.

Chapter 31
Common Simple Problems

Blisters

Those fluid-filled bubbles are mild second-degree burns caused by friction. The friction produces a separation of the tough outer layer of our skin from the sensitive inner layer. Only where skin is callused is it thick enough for this to happen—heels, soles, palms. Other skin just wears away with friction, leaving an abrasion.

The space between the outer layer of the blister (the roof) and the inner layer (the base) fills with fluid drawn from our circulatory system to protect the damaged area while it heals. Gravity encourages this to happen and causes foot blisters to swell rapidly. Wet skin blisters much more quickly than dry skin, and warm skin more quickly than cool skin. And what skin is more moist and hot than our feet in heavy boots after a long walk?

What should you do? Blisters heal faster when the fluid is drained, three to four times faster. Besides, they feel better when the bubble is deflated. Clean around the site thoroughly with soap and water, and rinse. In a flame, sterilize the tip of a knife, or use a sterile scalpel. Carefully slice the blister open and let it drain until the fluid is gone. Leaving the roof intact will let it feel better and mend quicker. If the roof has already been rubbed away when you discover the injury, treat the wound initially as you would any other—clean it and keep it clean to prevent infection.

Now the idea is to reduce the friction on that area as much as possible while keeping the foot in the field. Put a glob of gooey antiseptic on the deflated blistr. A povidone-iodine ointment works very well. Cover the site with a thick gauze pad, or build a moleskin "doughnut." Tape the gauze or moleskin securely in place. A liberal application of tincture of benzoin compound on the skin before the moleskin or tape will greatly increase the stick-to-it-ness of both materials. If you run srips of tape along the sides of the foot, toward the toes, then tape down the ends with strips that run around the instep, your efforts will outlast the abuse further travel puts on the system. A product called 2ND Skin works as well or better to reduce friction over a deflated blister. 2ND Skin also requires tape (or moleskin) to hold it in place.

Figure 31-1
Bandaging a blister.

You may never need these dirctions if you take precautions to prevent blisters from forming. Of critical importance is the fit of your boots. It doesn't matter how expensively your feet are shod if the fit is poor. Fit your boots with the socks you intend to wear in them. Boots that are the right size and are well broken in go a long way toward preventing blisters.

Keeping your feet cool and dry is important. Take frequent breaks with your boots off. Wear a thin liner sock that wicks moisture away from your feet and into a thicker outer sock. Some folks report success from applications of anti-perspirants to their feet. Most people think it makes their feet sticky, which increases friction. Some foot powders help reduce moisture and friction, but they also tend to cake up and require frequent applications.

Listen to your feet. When you hear a "hot spot" developing, stop and cover the area with tape or moleskin or 2nd Skin before the blister has a chance to form. Moleskin will conform to the shape of your feet better if you cut it into strips first instead of laying down a wide piece that inevitably refuses to go flat. Once again, tincture of benzoin compound applied first will help keep the tape or moleskin from peeling off when your feet start sweating.

Without tape or moleskin, benzoin can be applied to the skin of feet to prevent blisters. Benzoin hardens the outer layers of skin, and can be applied to hands also to prevent blisters that result from long hours of paddling.

Constipation

Constipation is a plug in the system usually created by either a fluid level too low to lubricate the tract, a fiber level too low to keep things rolling along, or a poor attitude concerning squatting over a cathole. Constipation can be encouraged by poor exercise habits.

Treatment should start with forcing fluids. Encourage the sufferer to eat lots of whole grains, fruits (dried is okay), and vegetables. Peanut butter, cheese and high-fat foods should be avoided. If you are prone to the problem, add a stool softener to your first-aid kit. Refrain from using the stronger medications for constipation. They can result in explosive deliveries and heavy fluid loss.

Someone who hasn't had a bowel movement in five days could be developing serious problems from the toxins building up in their intestinal tract. They should be considered for evacuation. When evacuation is not an immediate option, it might be necessary to go in with an index finger, break up the impaction, and pull it out. Disgusting as it may sound, it might prove lifesaving.

Prevention of constipation is essentially the same as with diarrhea. Drink plenty of water, eat healthy. For those who have trouble going without a porcelain toilet, try picking a secluded spot with a scenic view and a minimum of tickling grasses . . . and practice.

Dental Emergencies

He was in pain. He was not in the least bit happy. When I paddled my canoe alongside, his lip had already puffed out as far as his nose, and the broken piece of his tooth lay in his open palm. For Robert, it was a lesson in choosing your paddling partner more carefully. For me, it was a stimulus to learn some basic dentistry for the field.

Backcountry tooth care can be divided into three categories: 1) prevention, 2) oral irritations, and 3) severe tooth pain. Being prepared for outdoor toothaches can mean finishing the day's fishing trip, the weekend's hike or the extended expedition in relative comfort, instead of sacrificing the fun to a throbbing jaw.

PREVENTION: See your dentist regularly, and at least 30 days before an extended trip, giving yourself time to have any discovered problems fixed. Routine oral hygiene includes brushing with a soft nylon bristle toothbrush. Try to eat apples, carrots or celery regularly. These fibrous fruits and vegetables after a meal help scrape teeth clean. And don't forget to floss, cleaning where the brush can't reach.

ORAL IRRITATIONS: Aside from the occasional swat across the mouth with a careless paddle, most people first notice dental pain while eating. The discomfort is often elicited when cold, sweets or your tongue hits where a filling has fallen out. Gently clean the area, removing any food that may be trapped in the tooth. Dip a cotton pellet in oil of cloves (eugenol) and swab out the vacancy. The pain should be soothed, but to ensure longer-lasting results, mix a little zinc oxide powder with a few drops of oil of cloves and stir the stuff until it becomes a paste. Push the paste into the hole. Or, even better, carry a tube of Cavit in your first-aid kit. A squeeze of the tube sends a bit of pre-mixed paste onto your finger. Roll it into a ball and place it where the filling used to be. Bite it softly into shape. Sugarless gum (chewed to softness), ski wax or candle wax can sometimes be successfully used to plug the hole where a filling fell out. All of these temporary fillings will wash out, requiring you to monitor each regularly. If you're a long way from a dentist, simply replace the temporary filling when the old one comes out. This same procedure can be followed if you break off a piece of a tooth exposing the underlying structures, producing pain.

A generalized soreness of the mouth, usually centering in the gums, is often due to poor oral hygiene. This condition should first be treated with salt water rinses (teaspoon of salt in glass of water three to four times a day) and aggressive tooth brushing. If the condition persists, see a dentist for therapy.

SEVERE DENTAL PAIN: I believe my teeth are connected directly to my pain center. Aches in other parts of my body I can usually ignore. But screeching toothaches demand complete attention. Infection, exposure of the tooth's pulp, exposure of arteries, veins or nerves can create a screamer.

If the tooth is knocked out, pick it up by the top, not the root. Rinse it off, but don't scrub it. Your best chance of saving the fang is by pushing it gently back into the hole from whence it came. Once there, keeping your mouth shut will hold it in place until a dentist can be found. If it hurts, or refuses to go back in, don't force it. Wrap it in sterile gauze, and hold it in your mouth if possible, but keep it safe for the dental surgeon to attempt a replacement later. A piece of tooth broken off by trauma should likewise be saved. If a blow to the mouth has simply loosened a tooth, don't wiggle it until it firms up or a dentist is found. Never put an aspirin on the gum next to an aching tooth. This will cause an acid burn of the gum. It can be severe. Swallow the aspirin, or another pain killer, if you need relief. If, however, tooth pulp is exposed, a tiny piece of aspirin placed directly on the pulp will "cauterize the wound"— expect fierce pain followed by blessed relief.

Infection is indicated by a lot of swelling of the gum and cheek around an aching tooth. Gas and pus can be trapped inside the gum, causing extreme pain. If the swelling from infection reaches a major stage, the gum may form an elevated bulge that can turn blue. The patient needs antibiotics and a dentist. Ice packs on the jaw will help alleviate pain. If evacuation is not possible, you might have to consider a gentle slice with a sterile point to release the pressure and drain the infection. This is dangerous and not advisable except in radical circumstances. Likewise, attempting to pull a tooth out of an infected socket is dangerous. Both can cause significant bleeding.

Any bleeding inside the mouth, for any reason, can be given direct pressure. You can do this with a gauze pad you have bitten to hold in place. A moistened tea bag (non-herbal) can be used instead of gauze, and may work better. The tannic acid in tea initiates the formation of clotting. Avoid irritating the wound, which can renew the bleeding. Irritants are smoking, extremely hot food, chewing on the "bad" side, and sucking on the wound site.

If a crown breaks off a tooth, clean the crown and coat it with a little oil of cloves. Place it back on the tooth to see if it can be fitted properly. Remove again, and put a dab of Cavit on the crown. Set it immediately back in place, and bite it gently into position. If it won't fit, pack the tooth with dental wax until you can find a dentist.

A friendly dentist, outdoorsperson or not, should be willing to help you in finding and learning how to use the first-aid items specific to dental problems. Some excellent commercial backcountry dental kits are available.

Dehydration

It looks like you're going to walk right across the sky. The ridge sweeps up into the blue, making you want to just keep climbing. Below, the water of the lake glitters in the sun, spreading out like a sea. Water, water, everywhere, as the Ancient Mariner said, but no drop to drink up here. The water bottle has been forgotten. It is lying by the tent, back in camp.

Tongues are hanging out, and the water down in the lake smiles up, adding weight to the misery. The thirst being suffered is a sign that the internal fluid level is already low. The nag of a dry mouth means refreshment should have been swallowed long ago. Not especially because you want to, but because you know you need to. Dehydration is probably the major cause of feeling unhealthy in the outdoors.

More of your body is water than not. And that fluid is constantly being lost through urination, respiration, sweating, even crying. The loss is aggravated if you develop diarrhea, vomiting, or bleeding from a nasty wound. You need to maintain your personal water table in order to stay healthy. Hydrate or die!

What does water do? It keeps the pressure balanced in and out of your cells so you metabolize nutrients more efficiently and thus have more energy. Your kidneys need it to function properly. Otherwise, some of their workload is dumped on your liver, and metabolism slows down even more. Brains are very sensitive to water level changes, making dehydration one of the primary sources of headache. Lack of sufficient internal water may lead to poor bowel activity, resulting in constipation. With dehydration, your blood volume declines and you're set up for the cold weather problems of hypothermia and frostbite. Water is required to keep the sweating mechanism running smoothly, which allows you to stay cool on the hottest day.

Beyond thirst, fatigue and headache, your urine output will show that you're dehydrated. It should be ample, and clear or light yellow in color. If you haven't gone for a while, and your urine is dark yellow or orange, you're dehydrated. Advanced signs of water deficiency include lightheadedness and increased heart rate, especially when you first rise from a sitting position. If it goes far enough, your brain will fail to function properly.

How much water do you need? On the average, everyone should drink at least two liters per day. Water intake should be increased if it's hot and dry, and if you are at higher altitudes. While exercising, your need for water grows extreme. The recommended drinking regimen for periods of exercise requires discipline: 1) Down 500 milliliters (a half liter) before starting out, and 2) drink 250-300 milliliters approximately every 20 minutes during exercise. Cold water is absorbed faster than warm water. Water that contains about 6-7% carbohydrate (e.g. sports drinks) is absorbed faster than plain water. And those of us who are overweight need more water. Incidentally, drinking lots of water helps reduce your weight, not increase it.

If you drink more than you need, it simply means a few more trips to the bushes. Coffee, tea and non-decaffeinated soft drinks are not satisfactory. They increase fluid loss. Alcohol is especially counter-productive. It draws water out of your cells to dilute the increasing toxicity of your blood. Don't mistakenly think your body will draw all the water it needs from the food you eat. Although we do take in fluid that way, the best source of water is water.

Diarrhea

Diarrhea, the word, comes from the Greek for "a flowing through." Diarrhea, the distress, can come from viruses, bacteria (as in food poisoning), protozoa (like Giardia), and just being very anxious. It can be mild, moderate or severe depending on the frequency of the run to the bushes, the pain of cramping, the vileness of gas (judge for yourself), and the wateriness of the bowel movement. The problem can last from six hours to many weeks.

Initial treatment for all diarrhea is essentially the same. Discover what is causing the problem and quit swallowing it (if applicable), and replace the fluids that are being lost. For fluid replacement, clear liquids are the best choice: water, broth, herbal teas, fruit juices you can see through. The diarrhea should go away in about a day.

For a more persistent problem, start replacing the electrolytes that are being lost with the diarrhea. Commercially prepared mixes can be carried in your first-aid kit (e.g. oral rehydration salts), or you can create a field remedy: 1) To one liter of fruit juice or fruit drink (the potassium content needs to be high) add a tablespoon of sugar or honey (necessary for salt absorption) and a teaspoon of salt. 2) To a second liter of water add one teaspoon of baking soda. The patient should drink about one-fourth of each solution every hour, along with all the water he'll tolerate.

Non-prescription anti-diarrhea tablets (e.g. Imodium) can be carried in your first-aid kit, and used with relative safety (read the label). On extended trips, stronger medications might be advisable, but get advice from your doctor.

Treatment can be augmented by controlling what the sufferer eats. If the diarrhea is persistent, stick to liquids. As the problem subsides, start eating bland foods such as toast, crackers, pasta, rice, potatoes, and avoid spices, alcohol, coffee, fruits, hard cheeses and other fat-laden foods. As the future brightens, add meats and vegetables, but continue to go easy on the irritating foods.

Evacuation is seldom required, but should be undertaken if the patient persistently vomits, develops a fever, complains of localizing burning pain, or produces dark or black blood in the stool or vomit.

Help prevent diarrhea by maintaining a backcountry diet high in fiber and low in fat. Drink plenty of water, and take precautions to ensure it is disinfected by heating, filtering or iodizing. Wash your hands before preparing food, and clean up the kitchen gear after meals.

Gas

Passing gas through the rectum (flatus) is usually a relief and often a pleasant experience for the passer. If it becomes a problem, the distress will likely be social instead of medical. Heavy collections of gas can become painful, especially at higher altitudes. An easing of the pain is possible with an antacid containing the drug simethicone, available over the counter.

Headache

A common outdoor complaint, headaches have three general causes: 1) dehydration, 2) muscular tension, and 3) a vascular disorder. Most headaches respond to rest, hydration, massage, and over-the-counter medications (e.g. ibuprofen). Beware the headache that comes on suddenly, is unrelieved by normal treatment, and is not like any other headache you've ever had. Find a doctor.

Motion Sickness

For those who suffer the trip-ruining affliction of motion sickness, a dose of meclizine 25 milligrams about one hour prior to shoving off should calm the internal waves. Minimal side-effects, including drowsiness, will be experienced. Those who really suffer should ask for a presciption of Transderm Scop (scopalamine). Each expensive Scop patch can be worn behind the ear for three days of freedom from sickness.

Nausea and Vomiting

It can come from something you ate, something you smelled, or a serious underlying illness. Typically it is just the body's way of dealing with something that is upsetting the normal balance. Problems usually resolve within 24 hours, but the patient can be treated with an over-the-counter drug—meclizine 25 milligrams every eight hours. Nausea would deserve evacuation if it produced persistent vomiting, especially if there were dark "coffee grounds" blood in the vomit. Reasons for concern also include localized pain and high fever in an overly anxious patient.

Snowblindness

Six to 12 hours after overexposure to the sun's ultraviolet radiation, to which you're especially susceptible as it bounces off snow, your eyes feel painful, like "eyes full of sand." The cornea of the eye has been sunburned, and it is very sensitive to light. You're not truly "blind," but practically so, because it hurts so much to open up those peepers. Cool, wet compresses may be applied for pain. A small amount of anitbiotic ointment may be applied several times a day for two to three days. Pull down the bottom lid, apply a thin coating, blink a few times, and keep still with eyes shut till the ointment melts. If possible, don't use the eyes for 24 hours. Snowblindness almost always resolves harmlessly in 24-48 hours. Prolonged discomfort would be reason to come off the mountain and find a physician. Problems can be prevented by wearing sunglasses that block all, or almost all, UV light. On snow or water, sunglasses should fit well and have side-shields to block reflected light.

Splinters

Splinters should be removed as soon as possible. If the end is visible, grasp it with tweezers and pull it gently out. If the end is buried, probe with your fingers until you find the orientation of the splinter, and push it toward the opening of the wound until the end is graspable. With deeply buried splinters, you may need to cut superficially, preferably with a sterile scalpel from your first-aid kit, to expose the embedded object. Wash and apply antibiotic ointment to any wounds left after removal.

Sunburn

The immediate response to overexposure to ultraviolet light is burned skin. Prolonged exposure, over years, leads to premature skin aging and degenerative skin disorders, such as cancer. First aid for sunburn includes cooling the skin, applying a moisturizer, ibuprofen for pain and inflammation, and staying out of direct sunlight. Sunburn almost always self-limits, but if blisters form, a doctor should be consulted. Prevention of sunburn includes hats with brims and tightly-woven clothing, sunblocks such as zinc oxide on sensitive areas, and sunscreens, applied before exposure, with a high sun protection factor—SPF 15 or more. Be aware: You can burn on cloudy days; sunlight is most harmful between the hours of 10AM and 3PM; and large amounts of UV light are reflected dangerously back at you by snow and water.

Water Disinfection

Finding enough potable liquid in the backcountry can be a problem. If you don't carry it all in with you, there are three other ways to obtain safe water: death to germs by heat, by halogenation with iodine or chlorine, and by filtration.

Heat is an excellent disinfecting process. If the water is heated until it rolls, the heat is enough to kill the protozoa, bacteria and viruses that harm humans, around the world, up to 19,000 feet above sea level.

Iodine is generally a little safer halogen bet than chlorine on a long backcountry trip. It combines less eagerly with organic matter in water. To be sure water is safe to drink after treating it with iodine or chlorine, you have to consider variables such as temperature and clarity. Instead of risking a bout with some gastrointestinal illness, buy a bottle of water-disinfecting tablets or crystals and follow the directions on the label. You can also use the povidone-iodine in your first-aid kit—eight drops of solution in warm clear water and a 15-minute wait will give you a safe drink. In cold clear water, double the drops and double the wait.

WATER DISINFECTION

SUBSTANCE	AMOUNT USED	CONTACT TIME
Laundry Bleach 4% to 6% solution	2 drops/quart............	Let Stand 30 Minutes
Water should have a slight chlorine odor; if not, repeat dose and let stand an additional 15 minutes		
Halazone Tablets	5 tablets/quart	Let Stand 30 Minutes
Defective halazone tablets have an objectionable odor.		
Tincture of Iodine 2% solution	5 drops/quart .... clear water 10 drops/quart cloudy water	Let Stand 30 Minutes
Potable Aqua (globuline tetraglycine hydroperiodide)	1 tablet/quart............ if very cold 1 tablet/quart .... clear water 1 tablet/quart .... cloudy water	Let Stand 10 Minutes Let Stand 20 Minutes Let Stand 30 Minutes

Crystals of iodine can also be used to prepare a saturated iodine-water solution for use in disinfecting drinking water. Four to eight grams of USP grade iodine crystals can be placed in a one-ounce glass bottle. Water added to this bottle will dissolve an amount of iodine based upon its temperature. It is this saturated iodine-water solution which is then added to the quart of water. The amount added to produce a final concentration of four parts per million will vary according to temperature as indicated in the chart above.

This water should be stored for 15 minutes before drinking. If the water is turbid, or otherwise contaminated, the amounts of saturated iodine solution indicated above should be doubled and the resultant water stored 20 minutes before using. This product is now commercially available as Polar Pure through many outdoor stores and catalog houses.

All backcountry water filters are not created equal. If you choose filtration as your method of getting safe water, be sure to check on the specific qualifications of your selected filter to do all the things you want it to do.

Some filters remove only protozoa such as Giardia and Cryptosporidium, some remove protozoa and bacteria. None filter out viruses (which are not a problem in most of the wilderness water in the United States), but some have an iodine resin on the filter that kills viruses (e.g. "Guardian" from SweetWater, Boulder, Colorado (303) 530-2715, and PUR "Explorer" from Recovery Engineering, Minneapolis, Minnesota (800) 845-7873).

> NOTE: For more information on simple problems and wilderness drug therapies (for simple and serious problems), refer to the most excellent work by William Forgey, M.D.: Wilderness Medicine, Fourth Edition, ICS BOOKS, Inc. (800) 541-7323.

Chapter 32
The Five Commandments
of First-Aid Kits

Number 1:

Thou shalt find it impossible to put together the perfect first-aid kit.

Go ahead and try, but eventually, if you spend enough time in the backcountry, you will one day wish for something that is not there. It is possible to create a kit to meet your every need—almost! But don't ever try to convince someone else that your choice of first-aid items is better than theirs. Accept the fact that these kits are very personal. You may get by for years on a small piece of moleskin because your feet are tough. Your partner may need a mile of the stuff for an overnight hike.

Not abiding by the First Commandment, here is a list of items for the "almost perfect" first-aid kit:

- A few adhesive strips. The ones that are somewhat resistant to water last longer, and the ones about one inch by three inches work in most situations. And a couple made specially to cover knuckles are nice, too.
- A few sterile gauze pads, around four inches by four inches. They'll cover larger ouchies, and can be cut down for smaller wounds, and doubled up for bigger ones. They can be used to scrub out dirtier injuries, or molded into a covering for an irritated eye.
- A roll of athletic tape, one inch by ten yards. It holds down the gauze, prevents blisters when applied to sensitive spots at the start of a trip, and repairs injured equipment for short periods of time. Athletic tape shapes itself more easily to the strange designs of human extremities, and can be used to supportively wrap ankles.

- Tincture of benzoin compound. When the benzoin is rubbed on skin before anything you want to stick is applied, it sticks better.
- Wound closure strips. They are for pulling together the sides of a clean wound that gapes open.
- An individually wrapped sanitary napkin. This lightweight, inexpensive item makes a wonderful compress for badly bleeding injuries. Or you can pack a real trauma dressing.
- Povidone-iodine. For cleaning wounds or disinfecting water.
- Moleskin and/or 2nd Skin. It works great to prevent blisters if applied before the damage is done, and to treat blisters so a trip can continue in more comfort after a bubble has developed and been drained.
- A few tablets of a painkiller (e.g. aspirin or ibuprofen). This medication can bring a bit of relief after you have grown a headache, a muscle or joint ache, a fever, or just about anything that causes painful discomfort.
- An elastic wrap and/or Coban. Can be used to compress strains and sprains for a little added comfort, or used to hold a possible broken bone to a splint, or used as a constricting band in the treatment of poisonous snakebite, or used to hold the compress on a bad bleed, or used in any other creative way you can think of.
- A couple of safety pins. They can secure the elastic wrap, be sterilized for puncturing a blister to drain it, repair rips in clothing, or whatever.
- A few mild antihistamine tablets. Benadryl is probably the best for most people. The tablets' sedative effect helps relieve the itch of allergies and insect bites, helps you get to sleep (so don't take one and continue a high-risk outdoor activity), and helps ease the symptoms of a cold (but antihistamines do not cure a runny nose, and possibly extend the cold's life by causing your body to forget to fight off the infection).
- A couple of tablets of Imodium for diarrhea.
- Antimicrobial ointment.
- Scissors and tweezers are things you'll find yourself using on a daily basis in the backcountry. They can be a part of your pocketknife, which is the friendliest way to keep them ready for use.
- Rubber gloves.

Throw in other items depending on the time of year and the part of the country you're traveling through. Things like a dab of meat tenderizer to rub on serious insect bites, sunscreen, lip balm, more potent medications for specific problems, and the phone numbers of the closest emergency aid in case something really bad happens and you have to hurry out for help.

You have most likely already thought of things that should have been left out or included. Fine! Put them all in a bag, and carry it whenever you travel outdoors. A first aid kit is only useful if it is with you.

NOTE: Many excellent commercially prepared kits are available.

Number 2:

Thou shalt choose things for your first aid kit that are versatile rather than specific.

You do not need to carry on your back a variety of different sizes of band-aids, several widths of tape, three brands of painkillers (in their original bottles), and a wide range of thicknesses of gauze. Pack a few of the most commonly used items, and improvise when you need to.

Number 3:

Thou shalt not carry anything in your first-aid kit that you are not familiar with.

What's the point of packing along something you don't know how to use? Why carry a suture kit or prescription drugs unless you fully understand their uses? Besides, it could be dangerous for the person who needs first aid if you try to sew up a gaping woud, or give them some medications they can't tolerate.

Number 4:

Thou shalt re-pack your first-aid kit at least seasonally.

For one thing, there are expiration dates on many of those containers of medicinal supplies. And for another, moisture or heat or cold can creep in and destroy the efficacy of some of your items, and you'll never know it until you reach for them. Finally, lazy kit-checkers find they're carrying insect repellent on a winter trip where it is useless. Or rubbing alcohol on a ski excursion where it can be dangerous. What you include in your kit may also change when you explore a new geographic location.

Number 5:

Thou shalt not forget that the first-aid kit that saves lives rarely comes stuffed in a bag but in the human brain that stores skills.

Kits are mostly for the little trivial injuries that would probably be okay whether you interfere or not. Your ministrations can erase pain and speed healing, but it is knowledge and the ability to use that knowledge that makes the difference between life and death in a critical situation. Learn what you do for the seriously hurt or sick person, and carry that information with you all times.

Index